GREAT COOKING MADE EASY

COOKIES AND BISCUITS

Better Homes and Gardens
_{TRADEMARK}

TREASURE PRESS

BETTER HOMES AND GARDENS BOOKS

Editor Gerald M. Knox
Art Director Ernest Shelton
Managing Editor David A. Kirchner
Project Editors James D. Blume, Marsha Jahns
Project Managers Liz Anderson, Jennifer Speer Ramundt, Angela K. Renkoski

Cookies (American edition)
Editor Maureen Powers
Project Manager Marsha Jahns
Graphic Designer Lynda Haupert
Electronic Text Processor Paula Forest
Photographers Michael Jensen and Sean Fitzgerald
Food Stylists Suzanne Finley, Carol Grones, Dianna Nolin, Janet Herwig

Cookies and Biscuits (British edition)
Project Manager Liz Anderson
Assistant Art Director Tom Wegner
Contributing Project Editors Irena Chalmers Books, Inc., and associates: Jean Atcheson, Irena Chalmers, Ann Chase, Mary Dauman, Cathy Garvey, Mary Goodbody, Terri Griffing, Margaret Homberg, Kathryn Knapp, Stephanie Lyness, Susan Anderson Nabel, Victoria Proctor, Elizabeth Wheeler
Electronic Text Processors Alice Bauman, Kathy Benz, Paula Forest, Vicki Howell, Mary Mathews, Joyce Wasson

This edition first published in Great Britain in 1989 by:

Treasure Press
Michelin House
81 Fulham Road
London, SW3 6RB

Original edition published by Meredith Corporation in the United States of America.

BETTER HOMES AND GARDENS is a registered trademark in Canada, New Zealand, South Africa, and other countries.

ISBN 1 85051 434 8

Produced by Mandarin Offset
Printed and bound in Hong Kong

Mmmm . . . there's nothing quite like the enticing aroma of warm cookies and biscuits. And nowhere has the lively art of biscuit baking been more creative than in the United States. Included in this book are versions of America's best homemade cookies, such as nut cookies, zesty spice cookies, or rich, dark chocolate cookies. Chewy and crisp, big and small, this collection of cookies and biscuits has it all.

In *Cookies and Biscuits,* you'll find the best drop cookies, bar biscuits, biscuit cones, cut-out cookies, and deep-fried biscuits that are so popular in America. With the helpful hints on cookie making we've included, baking batches of your favourite sweet treats will be even easier.

So come on! Savour the flavours and the sweet tastes of success with these sensational recipes.

Contents

No-Bake Goodies

"Just what do you make of it, Watson? Are these no-bake beauties cookies or sweets? Or both?"

You don't have to be Sherlock Holmes to solve this luscious puzzler. Their double identity lets them be whatever you want—cookie *or* sweet.

So when you're tracking clues, searching for a super-simple, no-fuss, fix-'em-fast treat, start here.

Happy Birthday Miss Clavelle

Crisp Peanut Balls and Choco-Peanut Squares

Crisp Peanut Balls

4 **ounces (110g) caster sugar**
4 **fluid ounces (110ml) golden syrup**
9 **ounces (250g) peanut butter**
1½ **ounces (40g) crisp rice cereal**

Line a baking tray with greaseproof paper. Set aside. Combine sugar and golden syrup. Cook and stir until sugar is dissolved (see photo 1). Stir in peanut butter until melted. Remove from heat. Add cereal, stirring until combined (see photo 2). Drop by rounded teaspoons onto the prepared baking tray. *Or*, shape into 1-inch (2.5cm) balls (see photo 3). Makes about 64.

Choco-Peanut Squares: Prepare Crisp Peanut Balls as above, *except* line a 9x9x2-inch (23x23x5cm) baking tin with foil, extending foil over edges of tin. Press cereal mixture into prepared tin (see photo 4). Sprinkle 6 ounces (175g) *finely chopped plain chocolate* over the top. Let stand for 5 minutes. Spread softened chocolate pieces over cereal mixture. Chill about 30 minutes. Lift cereal mixture out of tin. Peel off foil. Cut into squares. Makes 36.

1 As you cook the sugar and golden syrup mixture, stir it constantly, but gently, so it doesn't splash on the sides of the saucepan. When the sugar dissolves completely, no grains will be visible; the mixture will be a clear syrup, as shown.

2 Add the cereal to the tin a little bit at a time. That way, it all becomes well coated with the peanut butter mixture.

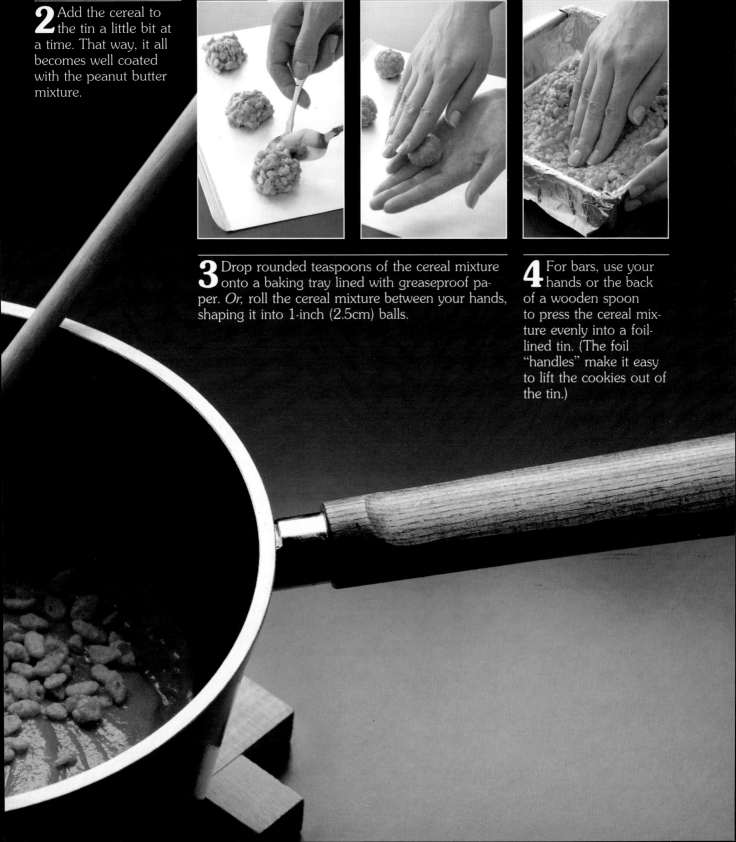

3 Drop rounded teaspoons of the cereal mixture onto a baking tray lined with greaseproof paper. *Or,* roll the cereal mixture between your hands, shaping it into 1-inch (2.5cm) balls.

4 For bars, use your hands or the back of a wooden spoon to press the cereal mixture evenly into a foil-lined tin. (The foil "handles" make it easy to lift the cookies out of the tin.)

Cinnamon-Marshmallow Squares

10   ounces (285g) marshmallows
2   ounces (50g) butter *or* margarine
2   ounces (50g) crisp rice cereal
1½   ounces (40g) cornflakes, slightly crushed
2   ounces (50g) cinnamon-flavoured sweets *or* raisins

Line a 9x9x2-inch (23x23x5cm) baking tin with foil, extending foil over the edges of the tin. Butter the foil. Set tin aside.

In a large saucepan melt marshmallows and butter or margarine over low heat, stirring constantly. Remove pan from heat. Add rice cereal, cornflakes, and cinnamon sweets or raisins, stirring until combined (see photo 2, page 9). Press mixture evenly into prepared tin (see photo 4, page 9). Let stand until firm. Use the foil to lift mixture out of tin. Peel off the foil. Cut into squares. Makes 18.

Tropical Fruit Balls

3   fluid ounces (80ml) thawed pineapple juice concentrate
3   tablespoons golden syrup
12   ounces (350g) finely crushed Nice biscuits (about 65 biscuits)
4   ounces (110g) chopped raisins
2   ounces (55g) chopped almonds, toasted
Sifted icing sugar *or* finely crushed Nice biscuits

In a large bowl stir together thawed concentrate and golden syrup. Add the 12 ounces (350g) crushed Nice biscuits, stirring until combined (see photo 2, page 9). Add raisins and almonds. Mix with hands until combined.

Shape the fruit mixture into 1-inch (2.5cm) balls (see photo 3, page 9). Roll balls in icing sugar or crushed biscuits to coat. Store tightly covered in the refrigerator. Makes about 60.

Chocolate Rum Balls

Make these dried fruit confections in advance and store them in the freezer for up to a month. Just before serving, spruce them up a bit by rerolling them in sugar.

2   fluid ounces (55ml) honey
3   tablespoons rum *or* orange juice
8   ounces (225g) chocolate-flavoured biscuits, finely crushed
6   ounces (175g) dried apricots, finely chopped
Caster sugar

In a large mixing bowl stir together honey and rum or orange juice. Add crushed biscuits and apricots, stirring until combined (see photo 2, page 9). Shape into 1-inch (2.5cm) balls (see photo 3, page 9). Roll balls in sugar. Makes about 40.

Rocky Road Drops

For a festive splash of colour, use coloured marshmallows in these sweet-like cookies, if you can find them.

6   ounces (175g) plain chocolate pieces
6   ounces (175g) chocolate- *or* vanilla-flavoured confectioners' coating, cut up
1½   ounces (40g) peanut butter cereal *or* rice cereal
1½   ounces (40g) tiny marshmallows
4   ounces (110g) peanuts

Line a baking tray with greaseproof paper. Set aside. In a medium heavy saucepan melt chocolate pieces and confectioners' coating over low heat, stirring often. Remove pan from heat.

In a medium mixing bowl stir together cereal, marshmallows, and peanuts. Add cereal mixture to melted chocolate, stirring until combined (see photo 2, page 9). Drop by rounded teaspoons onto the prepared baking tray (see photo 3, page 9). Chill about 1 hour or until firm. Store tightly covered in the refrigerator. Makes about 36.

Bar Arithmetic

Bars may be cut into a variety of shapes and sizes. The number of bars a recipe yields depends on the size of the tin as well as the size of the portion. As a general rule, the thicker the bar, the smaller it should be cut. Likewise, the richer the bar, the smaller the serving.

Use the table below as a guide for cutting bars. The size of the bar or square is approximate and will vary with your tins.

Baking Tin and Tray Sizes	Number of Cuts Lengthwise	Crosswise	Approximate Size of Bar	Number of Bars
8x8x2 in. (20x20x5cm)	3	3	2x2 in. (5x5cm)	16
	3	4	2x1½ in. (5x4cm)	20
	4	4	1½x1½ in. (4x4cm)	25
	3	7	2x1 in. (5x2.5cm)	32
9x9x2 in. (23x23x5cm)	2	5	3x1½ in. (7.5x4cm)	18
	3	5	2¼x1½ in. (5½x4cm)	24
	5	5	1½x1½ in. (4x4cm)	36
11x7x1½ in. (28x18x4cm)	3	3	1¾x2¾ in. (4.5x7cm)	16
	4	3	1⅜x2¾ in. (3x7cm)	20
	4	4	1⅜x2¼ in. (3x5½cm)	25
	3	7	1¾x1⅜ in. (4.5x3cm)	32
13x9x2 in. (32.5x23x5cm)	3	7	2¼x1⅝ in. (5½x4.2cm)	32
	5	5	1½x2⅛ in. (4x5cm)	36
	5	7	1½x1⅝ in. (4x4.2cm)	48
15x10x1 in. (38x25.5x2.5cm)	3	7	2½x1⅞ in. (6x4.5cm)	32
	3	11	2½x1¼ in. (6x3cm)	48
	7	8	1¼x1¾ in. (3x4.5cm)	72

Batter Bars And Brownies

Quick, easy, and irresistible—now that's a biscuit worth investing in. These priceless bars are gems because they require no rolling, no cutting, no dropping, and no shaping.

Simply stir together the batter for these yummy bars and brownies, and bake. You'll want to protect these jewels. But don't—it's fun sharing your wealth!

Citrus-Yogurt Squares

Citrus-Yogurt Squares

- **6 ounces (175g) plain flour**
- **1 teaspoon baking powder**
- **¼ teaspoon bicarbonate of soda**
- **3 ounces (75g) butter *or* margarine**
- **6 ounces (175g) caster sugar**
- **1 egg**
- **1 teaspoon finely grated lemon peel *or* orange peel**
- **4 teaspoons lemon juice *or* orange juice**
- **4 ounces (110g) natural, lemon, *or* orange yogurt**
- **4 ounces (110g) sifted icing sugar**

Grease a 9x9x2-inch (23x23x5cm) baking tin. Set aside. In a medium mixing bowl stir together flour, baking powder, and soda (see photo 1). Set aside.

In a medium saucepan melt butter or margarine. Remove from heat. Stir in sugar. Add egg, ½ *teaspoon* lemon peel or orange peel, and *1 teaspoon* lemon juice or orange juice. Beat well. Stir in yogurt (see photo 2). Gradually add flour mixture, beating till combined. Spread batter into the prepared tin (see photo 3).

Bake in a 350°F (180°C) gas mark 4 oven for 25 to 30 minutes or till a wooden toothpick inserted in centre comes out clean (see photo 4). Cool completely on a wire rack.

For glaze, in a small mixing bowl stir together icing sugar, remaining ½ teaspoon lemon peel or orange peel, and remaining 3 teaspoons lemon juice or orange juice. Spread glaze over top. Cut into squares (see photo 5). Makes 18.

1 Stir the dry ingredients together in a medium-size mixing bowl. Mix well to evenly distribute leavenings (baking powder and/or bicarbonate of soda) and spices.

2 Stir in the yogurt last, when there's no chance of it becoming too hot and breaking down. Vanilla essence is also added at the end so its flavour doesn't evaporate.

3 As you spread the batter into the prepared tin, make sure it's about the same distance from the top of the tin on all sides and that the centre is level with the edges. The bars will look more attractive and bake more evenly.

4 To tell if cake-like bars are done, stick a wooden toothpick near the centre of the bars. If the toothpick comes out clean, the bars are ready to come out of the oven.

5 So you don't end up with crooked bars and brownies, use a ruler to measure and mark the bars into the size pieces you want. Then stick in toothpicks so you know where to cut.

Some bars need to be cut while still warm to prevent cracking or shattering; others need to cool completely before cutting. Follow the directions given in each recipe.

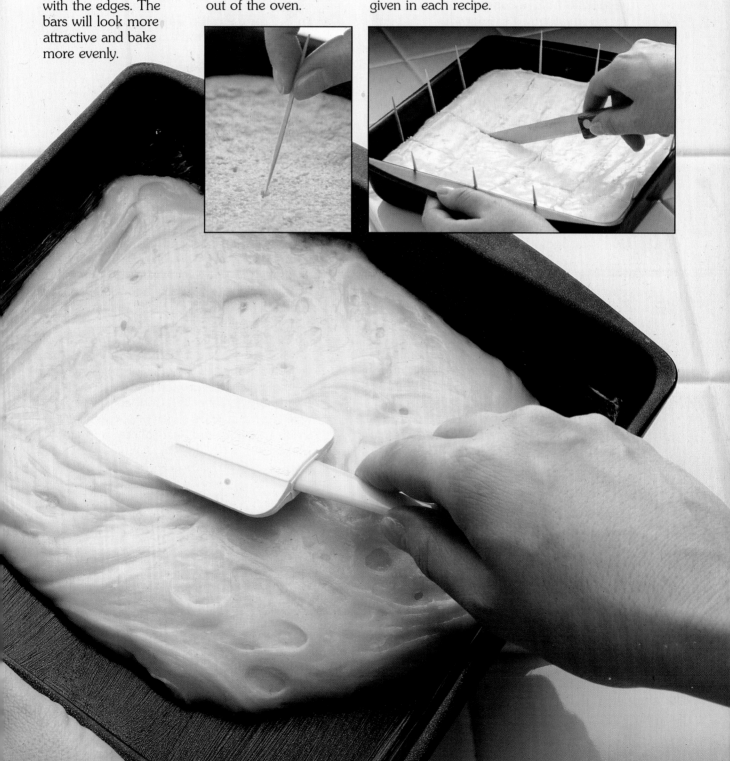

Carrot Bars

Complete with Cream Cheese Icing, these spicy bars are like tiny pieces of carrot cake.

 7 **ounces (200g) plain flour**
1½ **teaspoons baking powder**
1½ **teaspoons ground cinnamon**
 ¼ **teaspoon bicarbonate of soda**
 ¼ **teaspoon ground nutmeg**
 ⅛ **teaspoon ground cloves**
 3 **eggs**
 7 **ounces (200g) finely grated carrot**
 6 **ounces (175g) caster sugar**
 6 **fluid ounces (165ml) cooking oil**
 2 **ounces (50g) raisins**
 3 **ounces (75g) chopped walnuts**
   Cream Cheese Icing

In a medium mixing bowl stir together flour, baking powder, cinnamon, soda, nutmeg, and cloves (see photo 1, page 14). Set aside.

In a large mixing bowl combine eggs, carrot, sugar, and oil. Beat with an electric mixer until combined. Gradually add flour mixture, beating until combined. Stir in raisins and walnuts.

Spread the batter evenly into an ungreased 15x10x1-inch (43x25.5x2.5cm) baking tin (see photo 3, page 15). Bake in a 350°F (180°C) gas mark 4 oven for 25 to 30 minutes or until a wooden toothpick inserted in centre comes out clean (see photo 4, page 15). Cool completely on a wire rack.

Ice with Cream Cheese Icing. Cut into bars (see photo 5, page 15). Store tightly covered in the refrigerator. Makes 48.

Cream Cheese Icing: In a small mixing bowl beat 3 ounces (75g) *cream cheese,* softened; 2 ounces (50g) *butter or margarine;* and 2 to 3 drops *vanilla essence* with an electric mixer on medium speed until light and fluffy. Gradually beat in 8 ounces (225g) sifted *icing sugar* until smooth.

Maple-Walnut Bars

 5 **ounces (150g) plain flour**
 ½ **teaspoon baking powder**
2½ **ounces (60g) butter *or* margarine**
 3 **ounces (75g) caster sugar**
 1 **egg**
 2 **to 3 drops vanilla essence**
 3 **fluid ounces (80ml) maple-flavoured syrup**
 2 **fluid ounces (55ml) milk**
 3 **ounces (75g) chopped walnuts**
   Icing sugar (optional)

Grease a 9x9x2-inch (23x23x5-cm) baking tin. Set aside. In a small mixing bowl stir together flour and baking powder (see photo 1, page 14). Set aside.

In a small mixing bowl beat butter or margarine with an electric mixer on medium speed for 30 seconds. Add sugar and beat until fluffy (see photo 1, page 31). Add egg and vanilla and beat well. Beat in syrup and milk (mixture will appear curdled). Gradually add flour mixture, beating until combined. Stir in walnuts.

Spread batter into the prepared tin (see photo 3, page 15). Bake in a 350°F (180°C) gas mark 4 oven for 25 to 30 minutes or until a wooden toothpick inserted in centre comes out clean (see photo 4, page 15). Cool completely on a wire rack. Sift icing sugar over cookies, if desired. Cut into bars (see photo 5, page 15). Makes 24.

Chocolate Syrup Brownies

A mere 15 minutes in the kitchen and you can have rich, fudgy brownies ready to pop into the oven. In another 45 minutes or so, you can enjoy one with a glass of cold milk.

 6 **ounces (175g) plain flour**
 ¼ **teaspoon salt**
 4 **ounces (110g) butter *or* margarine**
 6 **ounces (175g) caster sugar**
 4 **eggs**
16 **ounces (460g) chocolate-flavoured syrup**
 5 **ounces (150g) chopped nuts**
 Quick Chocolate Glaze

In a small mixing bowl stir together flour and salt (see photo 1, page 14). Set aside.

In a large mixing bowl beat butter or margarine with an electric mixer for 30 seconds. Add sugar and beat until fluffy (see photo 1, page 31). Add eggs and beat well. Stir in chocolate-flavoured syrup. Gradually stir in flour mixture (mixture will appear curdled). Stir in nuts.

Spread batter into an ungreased 13x9x2-inch (32.5x23x5cm) baking tin (see photo 3, page 15). Bake in a 350°F (180°C) gas mark 4 oven for 30 to 35 minutes or until a wooden toothpick inserted in centre comes out clean (see photo 4, page 15). Cool slightly on a wire rack. Top with Quick Chocolate Glaze. Cool completely. Cut into bars (see photo 5, page 15). Makes 32.

Quick Chocolate Glaze: In a medium saucepan combine 4 ounces (110g) *caster sugar,* 3 tablespoons *milk,* and 3 tablespoons *butter or margarine.* Cook and stir over medium heat until mixture is boiling. Boil for 30 seconds. Remove from heat. Stir in 3 ounces (75g) *plain chocolate pieces* until melted.

Chewy Ginger Bars

10 **ounces (275g) plain flour**
 2 **teaspoons baking powder**
 1 **teaspoon ground ginger**
 1 **teaspoon ground cinnamon**
 ¼ **teaspoon ground cloves**
 4 **ounces (110g) butter *or* margarine**
11 **ounces (300g) soft brown sugar**
 2 **eggs**
 2 **fluid ounces (55ml) black treacle**
 2 **or 3 drops vanilla essence**
 Icing sugar

Grease a 13x9x2-inch (32.5x23x5cm) baking tin. Set aside. In a large mixing bowl stir together flour, baking powder, ginger, cinnamon, and cloves (see photo 1, page 14). Set aside.

In a saucepan melt butter or margarine. Remove from heat. Stir in soft brown sugar. Add eggs, one at a time, stirring until combined. Stir in black treacle and vanilla essence. Gradually add flour mixture, stirring until combined.

Spread batter into the prepared tin (see photo 3, page 15). Bake in a 350°F (180°C) gas mark 4 oven for 20 to 25 minutes or until a wooden toothpick inserted in centre comes out clean (see photo 4, page 15). Cool completely on a wire rack. Sift icing sugar over top. Cut into bars (see photo 5, page 15). Makes 32.

Butterscotch Blonde Brownies

If available, add butterscotch pieces to these brownies for a double-delicious dose of butterscotch flavour.

  8 **ounces (225g) plain flour**
  2 **ounces (50g) quick-cooking rolled oats**
  2 **teaspoons baking powder**
  4 **ounces (110g) butter *or* margarine**
 12 **ounces (350g) soft brown sugar**
  2 **eggs**
  2 **or 3 drops vanilla essence**
  3 **ounces (75g) chopped walnuts *or* pecans**
  3 **ounces (75g) butterscotch-flavoured pieces *or* plain chocolate pieces**
  1 **ounce (25g) coconut**

Grease a 13x9x2-inch (32.5x23x5cm) baking tin. Set aside. In a medium mixing bowl stir together flour, rolled oats, and baking powder (see photo 1, page 14). Set aside.

In a large saucepan melt butter or margarine. Remove from heat. Stir in sugar. Add eggs, one at a time, stirring until combined. Stir in vanilla essence (see photo 2, page 14).

Gradually add flour mixture, beating until combined. Stir in walnuts or pecans, butterscotch-flavoured pieces, and coconut. Spread batter into the prepared tin (see photo 3, page 15).

Bake in a 350°F (180°C) gas mark 4 oven for 20 to 25 minutes or until a wooden toothpick inserted in centre comes out clean (see photo 4, page 15). Cut into bars while warm (see photo 5, page 15). Cool completely on a wire rack. Makes 32.

Cocoa Cake Brownies

  8 **ounces (225g) plain flour**
  3 **ounces (75g) unsweetened cocoa powder**
  1 **teaspoon baking powder**
  ¼ **teaspoon bicarbonate of soda**
  6 **ounces (175g) butter *or* margarine**
  8 **ounces (225g) caster sugar**
  2 **eggs**
  2 **or 3 drops vanilla essence**
  8 **fluid ounces (220ml) milk**
  5 **ounces (150g) chopped walnuts**
     Cocoa Icing

Grease a 15x10x1-inch (37.5x25.5x2.5cm) baking tin. Set aside. In a medium mixing bowl stir together flour, cocoa powder, b powder, and soda (see photo 1, page 14). Set aside.

In a large mixing bowl beat butter or margarine with an electric mixer on medium speed for 30 seconds. Add sugar and beat until fluffy (see photo 1, page 31). Add eggs and vanilla essence and beat well. Add flour mixture and milk alternately to the beaten mixture, beating after each addition. Stir in walnuts.

Spread batter into the prepared tin (see photo 3, page 15). Bake in a 350°F (180°C) gas mark 4 oven about 18 minutes or until a wooden toothpick inserted in centre comes out clean (see photo 4, page 15). Cool completely on a wire rack. Frost with Cocoa Icing. Cut into bars (see photo 5, page 15). Makes 32.

Cocoa Icing: In a medium heavy saucepan combine 3 ounces (75g) *butter or margarine* and 3 tablespoons *milk*. Cook and stir over low heat until butter or margarine melts. Stir in 12 ounces (350g) sifted *icing sugar* and 1 ounce (25g) *unsweetened cocoa powder,* sifted. Add additional *milk,* if necessary, to make icing spreadable.

▶ *Pictured opposite: Butterscotch Blonde Brownies and Cocoa Cake Brownies*

Bars with A Crust

As the cookie foreman of your baking crew, it's your job to oversee the construction of these cookies—beginning with their tasty foundation.

A rich cookie crust supports the tempting topping on these oh-so-scrumptious bars.

When the cookies are finished baking, call in the wrecking crew to help demolish a whole plate of them.

Apricot Bars

Apricot Bars

3	ounces (75g) dried apricots, snipped
4	fluid ounces (110ml) water
1½	ounces (40g) soft brown sugar
1	tablespoon plain flour
½	teaspoon ground coriander
1	or 2 drops vanilla *essence*
4	ounces (110g) plain flour
3	ounces (75g) soft brown sugar
1½	ounces (40g) quick-cooking rolled oats
1	ounce (25g) whole bran cereal
3	ounces (75g) butter *or* margarine
3	tablespoons water

In a small saucepan combine the dried apricots and the 4 fluid ounces (110ml) water. Bring to boiling. Reduce heat and simmer, covered, for 8 to 10 minutes or until tender.

Meanwhile, combine the 1½ ounces (40g) soft brown sugar, the 1 tablespoon flour, and coriander. Stir into apricot mixture. Cook and stir until thickened (see photo 1). Remove from heat and stir in vanilla essence (see photo 2, page 14).

For crust, in a medium mixing bowl stir together the 4 ounces (110g) flour, the 3 ounces (75g) brown sugar, oats, and bran cereal. Cut in butter or margarine until crumbly (see photo 2). Reserve *4 to 5 ounces* (110 to 150g) of the crust mixture for topping. Stir the 3 tablespoons water into the remaining crust mixture.

Press crust mixture into the bottom of an ungreased 8x8x2-inch (20x20x5cm) baking tin (see photo 3). Spread apricot mixture evenly over crust (see photo 4). Sprinkle reserved crust mixture over the top, pressing in lightly. Bake in a 350°F (180°C) gas mark 4 oven for 30 to 35 minutes or until golden. Cool completely and cut into bars (see photo 5, page 15). Makes 25.

1 Cook the apricot mixture over low heat till it becomes very thick. Stir constantly, using a figure-8 motion, to prevent sticking and scorching, and to help the mixture cook evenly.

2 With a pastry blender or fork, use an up-and-down motion to mix the butter or margarine into the flour-oat mixture. Stop once in a while to scrape off any butter that sticks to the pastry blender or fork.

3 For bars with a crumb or dough crust, press the mixture into the tin with your hands. Make sure it's the same thickness in all areas for even baking.

4 Pour the apricot mixture over the crust. Using a spoon, spread it evenly to the edges.

Luscious Lemon Diamonds

3	ounces (75g) butter *or* margarine
1½	ounces (40g) caster sugar
½	teaspoon finely grated lemon peel
5	ounces (150g) plain flour
6	eggs
9	ounces (250g) caster sugar
1	teaspoon finely grated lemon peel
½	cup lemon juice
2	tablespoons plain flour
1	teaspoon baking powder
	Icing sugar

Grease an 11x7x1½-inch (28x18x4cm) baking tin. Set aside. For crust, beat butter with an electric mixer for 30 seconds. Add the 1½ ounces (40g) sugar and the ½ teaspoon lemon peel; beat until fluffy (see photo 1, page 31). Gradually add the 5 ounces (150g) flour; beat until crumbly. Press crust mixture evenly into the bottom of the prepared tin (see photo 3, page 23). Bake in a 350°F (180°C) mark 4 gas oven for 20 minutes.

Beat eggs, sugar, the 1 teaspoon lemon peel, lemon juice, the 2 tablespoons flour, and baking powder until combined. Continue beating about 3 minutes or until slightly thickened (mixture may be foamy). Spread evenly over hot crust (see photo 4, page 23). Return to oven; bake about 25 minutes more or until set. Cool. Just before serving, sift icing sugar over top. Cut into diamonds (see tip, below). Makes about 25.

Chocolate-Walnut Bars

4	ounces (110g) butter *or* margarine
2	tablespoons caster sugar
7½	ounces (210g) plain flour
2	eggs
3	ounces (75g) soft brown sugar
2½	ounces (60g) chopped walnuts
3	ounces (75g) plain chocolate pieces
4	fluid ounces (110ml) golden syrup
2	tablespoons butter *or* margarine, melted
2	or 3 drops vanilla essence

For crust, in a mixing bowl beat the 4 ounces (110g) butter or margarine with an electric mixer on medium speed for 30 seconds. Add caster sugar and beat until fluffy (see photo 1, page 31). Stir in flour. Press crust mixture evenly into the bottom of an ungreased 11x7x1½-inch (28x18x3cm) baking tin (see photo 3, page 23). Bake in a 350°F (180°C) gas mark 4 oven 15 minutes.

Meanwhile, in a medium mixing bowl beat eggs slightly. Stir in brown sugar, walnuts, chocolate pieces, golden syrup, the 2 tablespoons melted butter or margarine, and vanilla essence. Spread mixture evenly over hot crust (see photo 4, page 23). Return to oven and bake about 25 minutes more or until set. Cool on a wire rack. Cut into bars (see photo 5, page 15). Makes 25.

Cutting Biscuits Down to Size

Make your biscuit dish a little more interesting by cutting your bars into diamond or triangle shapes.
● To make triangles, simply cut bars into squares, then halve them diagonally.
● For diamonds, first make straight parallel cuts 1 to 1½ inches (2.5 to 3cm) apart down the length of your tin. Then make diagonal cuts across the tin (at a 45-degree angle), keeping the lines as even as you can. (You will have irregularly shaped pieces at each end of the tin. Use these to fill in small gaps on your biscuit plate.)

Orange-Raisin Bars

No food processor? Run the fruit and nut mixture through the coarse plate of a food grinder instead.

1	medium orange
2½	ounces (60g) raisins
2½	ounces (60g) walnuts
6	ounces (175g) butter *or* margarine
4½	ounces (125g) soft brown sugar
12½	ounces (360g) plain flour
1	tablespoon baking powder
2	eggs
6	fluid ounces (165ml) milk
	Orange Butter Icing
48	walnut halves

Grease a 13x9x2-inch (32.5x23x5cm) baking tin. Set aside. Finely grate *¼ teaspoon* orange peel and reserve for icing. Halve the orange. Juice one half, reserving 2 fluid ounces (55ml) juice (add water, if necessary). Discard orange half. Cut up the remaining *unpeeled* orange half. Place cut-up orange, raisins, and the 2½ ounces (20g) walnuts in a food processor bowl. Cover and process until ground. Set aside.

For crust, beat butter or margarine with an electric mixer for 30 seconds. Add brown sugar and beat until fluffy (see photo 1, page 31). Gradually add flour, beating until crumbly. Press *11 ounces (300g)* of the crust mixture evenly into bottom of the prepared tin (see photo 3, page 23). Stir baking powder into remaining crust mixture. Add reserved orange juice, eggs, and milk, beating until combined. Stir in ground orange mixture. Spread mixture evenly over crust (see photo 4, page 23). Bake in a 375°F (190°C) gas mark 5 oven for 20 to 25 minutes or until brown. Cool completely on a rack. Spread with Orange Butter Icing. Cut into bars (see photo 5, page 15). Garnish each with a walnut half. Makes 48.

Orange Butter Icing: Beat 2 ounces (50g) *butter or margarine* until light and fluffy. Gradually add 5 ounces (150g) sifted *icing sugar,* beating well. Beat in 2 tablespoons *milk,* 2 to 3 drops *vanilla essence,* and reserved orange peel. Gradually beat in 5 ounces (150g) sifted *icing sugar.* (Beat in additional *milk,* if necessary, to make spreadable.)

Peanut-Oat Bars

3	ounces (75g) quick-cooking rolled oats
2½	ounces (60g) plain flour
3	ounces (75g) soft brown sugar
¼	teaspoon bicarbonate of soda
3	ounces (75g) butter *or* margarine, melted
3	ounces (75g) cream cheese, softened
2	ounces (50g) peanut butter
1½	ounces (40g) caster sugar
2	fluid ounces (55ml) milk
1	egg
3	ounces (75g) chopped peanuts
2	ounces (50g) plain chocolate pieces
2	teaspoons lard

For crust, in a medium mixing bowl stir together oats, flour, brown sugar, and bicarbonate of soda (see photo 1, page 14). Stir in the melted butter or margarine. Press the crust mixture evenly into the bottom of an ungreased 11x7x1½-inch (28x18x4cm) baking tin (see photo 3, page 23). Bake in a 350°F (180°C) gas mark 4 oven for 8 minutes, until light brown.

Meanwhile, in a small mixing bowl beat cream cheese and peanut butter with an electric mixer until smooth. Add sugar, milk, and egg and beat well. Stir in peanuts. Spread mixture evenly over hot crust (see photo 4, page 23). Return to oven and bake about 18 minutes more or until set. Cool on a wire rack for 5 minutes.

In a small heavy saucepan melt chocolate pieces and lard over low heat until smooth. Drizzle over entire surface. Chill thoroughly. Cut into bars (see photo 5, page 15). Store tightly covered in the refrigerator. Makes 25.

Coffee 'n' Cream Bars

2	ounces (50g) butter *or* margarine
1½	ounces (40g) caster sugar
2	tablespoons coffee liqueur
5	ounces (150g) plain flour
2	teaspoons instant coffee crystals
3	fluid ounces (80ml) whipping cream
3	eggs
6	ounces (175g) caster sugar
1	tablespoon plain flour
2	or 3 drops vanilla essence
½	teaspoon baking powder
2½	ounces (60g) finely chopped walnuts *or* pecans

For crust, in a small mixing bowl beat butter or margarine with an electric mixer on medium speed for 30 seconds. Add the 1½ ounces (40g) sugar and beat until fluffy (see photo 1, page 31). Add coffee liqueur and beat well. Stir in the 5 ounces (150g) flour. Press mixture evenly into the bottom of an ungreased 11x7x1½-inch (28x18x4cm) baking tin (see photo 3, page 23). Bake in a 350°F (180°C) gas mark 4 oven 12 minutes.

Meanwhile, in a large mixing bowl dissolve coffee crystals in whipping cream. Add eggs, the 6 ounces (175g) sugar, the 1 tablespoon flour, vanilla, and baking powder and beat well. Spread mixture evenly over hot crust (see photo 4, page 23). Sprinkle with chopped nuts.

Return to oven and bake for 20 to 25 minutes more or until set in centre. Cool completely on a wire rack. Cut into bars (see photo 5, page 15). Store tightly covered in refrigerator. Makes 25.

Mocha Cheesecake Bars

The biscuit-crumb crust softens slightly if you store these bars overnight.

8½	ounces (235g) finely crushed chocolate wafers (about 30 wafers) *or* langues de chat
2	ounces (50g) butter *or* margarine, melted
8	ounces (225g) cream cheese, softened
4	ounces (110g) caster sugar
2	fluid ounces (55ml) milk
3	tablespoons unsweetened cocoa powder
3	eggs
3	tablespoons strong coffee

Grease an 11x7x1½-inch (28x18x4cm) baking tin. Set aside. For crust, in a medium mixing bowl stir together crushed wafers and melted butter or margarine. Press crust mixture evenly into the bottom of the prepared tin (see photo 3, page 23).

In a small mixing bowl beat cream cheese until fluffy. Add sugar, milk, and cocoa powder and beat until combined. Add eggs and coffee, beating just until combined. *Do not overbeat.*

Spread cream cheese mixture evenly over crust (see photo 4, page 23). Bake in a 350°F (180°C) gas mark 4 oven for 30 to 35 minutes or until centre appears set. Cool on a wire rack. Chill thoroughly. Cut into bars (see photo 5, page 15). Makes 25.

▶ *Pictured opposite: Mocha Cheesecake Bars*

Delightful Drops

Step right up for one of the greatest treats on earth! As ringmaster of this cookie extravaganza, you'll please any crowd with these three-ring favourites.

In the centre ring, lover's of chewy cookies will ooh and aah at American-styled Old-Fashioned Chocolate Chippers. Soured Cream Apricot Drops tame those who prefer tender, cake-like cookies. And, for anyone who likes a crisp drop cookie, take a chance on Oatmeal Wheat Treats.

No clowning around, all three of these drop cookies promise a performance worthy of an encore.

*Old-Fashioned
Chocolate Chippers*

Old-Fashioned Chocolate Chippers

12½ ounces (360g) plain flour
 1 teaspoon bicarbonate of soda
 4 ounces (110g) butter *or* margarine
 4 ounces (110g) lard
 6 ounces (175g) soft brown sugar
 3 ounces (75g) caster sugar
 2 eggs
 3 or 4 drops vanilla *essence*
12 ounces (350g) plain chocolate pieces
 5 ounces (150g) chopped walnuts *or*
   pecans

In a medium mixing bowl stir together the flour and bicarbonate of soda (see photo 1, page 14). Set aside.

In a large mixing bowl beat butter or margarine and lard with an electric mixer on medium speed for 30 seconds. Add soft brown sugar and caster sugar and beat until fluffy (see photo 1). Add eggs and vanilla essence and beat well. Gradually add flour mixture, beating until combined. Stir in chocolate pieces and nuts.

Drop by rounded teaspoons 2 inches (5cm) apart onto an ungreased baking tray (see photo 2). Bake in a 375°F (190°C) gas mark 5 oven for 8 to 10 minutes or until bottoms are lightly browned (see photo 3). Cool on baking tray for 1 minute. Remove; cool completely on wire racks (see photo 4). Makes 60.

Oatmeal Chippers: Prepare Old-Fashioned Chocolate Chippers as above, *except use 7½ ounces (210g)* plain flour and add 6 ounces (175g) *quick-cooking rolled oats.*

Double-Wheat Chippers: Prepare Old-Fashioned Chocolate Chippers as above, *except use 5 ounces (150g)* plain flour and add 5 ounces (150g) *whole wheat flour* and 6 ounces (175g) *unprocessed wheat bran.*

1 Beat the butter or margarine and lard together until creamy. Add the sugars and continue beating until the mixture is light and fluffy, as shown. Use a rubber scraper to scrape the sides of the bowl.

2 Scoop up the dough in a spoon. Use the back of another spoon to push the dough off the spoon. *Or,* use a dough dropper, a tool like the one pictured. It's available at kitchen gadget shops. The dough will spread while it's baking, so drop the mounds about 2 inches (5cm) apart.

3 Drop cookies are done when the dough is set and the bottoms are lightly browned. For chocolate cookies, however, test for doneness by lightly touching the top of a cookie with your fingertip. If they're done, the imprint will be barely visible. If they're not done, the imprint will be large and the cookies will be doughy.

4 Use a pancake turner or wide metal spatula to transfer the cookies from the baking tray to wire racks. Don't store or ice the cookies until they're completely cooled.

Double-Chocolate Chunk Specials

12½	ounces (360g) plain flour
1	ounce (25g) unsweetened cocoa powder
1	teaspoon bicarbonate of soda
4	ounces (110g) butter *or* margarine
4	ounces (110g) lard
6	ounces (175g) soft brown sugar
3	ounces (75g) caster sugar
2	eggs
3 or 4	drops vanilla essence
8	ounces (225g) milk chocolate, coarsely chopped, *or* 12 ounces (350g) plain chocolate pieces

In a medium mixing bowl stir together flour, cocoa powder, and soda (see photo 1, page 14). Set aside.

In a large mixing bowl beat butter or margarine and lard with an electric mixer on medium speed for 30 seconds. Add soft brown sugar and caster sugar and beat until fluffy (see photo 1, page 31). Add eggs and vanilla essence and beat well. Gradually add flour mixture, beating until combined. Stir in milk chocolate or plain chocolate.

Drop by rounded teaspoons 2 inches (5cm) apart onto an ungreased baking tray (see photo 2, page 31). Bake in a 375°F (190°C) gas mark 5 oven about 8 minutes or until a slight finger imprint remains (see photo 3, page 31). Cool on baking tray for 1 minute. Remove and cool completely on wire racks (see photo 4, page 31). Makes about 60.

Apple Pie Cookies

All the mouth-watering flavours of Mum's homemade apple pie—right here in these tender cookies.

10	ounces (275g) plain flour
1	teaspoon baking powder
1	teaspoon ground cinnamon
¼	teaspoon bicarbonate of soda
¼	teaspoon ground nutmeg
⅛	teaspoon ground cloves
4	ounces (110g) butter *or* margarine
6	ounces (175g) caster sugar
2	eggs
1	large apple, peeled, cored, and grated
4	teaspoons caster sugar
¼	teaspoon ground cinnamon

Lightly grease a baking tray. Set aside. In a mixing bowl stir together flour, baking powder, the 1 teaspoon cinnamon, soda, nutmeg, and cloves (see photo 1, page 14). Set aside.

In a large mixing bowl beat butter or margarine with an electric mixer on medium speed for 30 seconds. Add the 6 ounces (175g) caster sugar and beat until fluffy (see photo 1, page 31). Add eggs and beat well. Stir in grated apple. Gradually add flour mixture, beating until all ingredients are combined.

Drop by rounded teaspoons 2 inches (5cm) apart onto the prepared baking tray (see photo 2, page 31). Stir together the 4 teaspoons caster sugar and the ¼ teaspoon cinnamon. Sprinkle cinnamon-sugar mixture over tops of dough.

Bake in a 375°F (190°C) gas mark 5 oven for 8 to 10 minutes or until bottoms are lightly browned (see photo 3, page 31). Cool on baking tray for 1 minute. Remove and cool on wire racks (see photo 4, page 31). Makes about 40.

Oatmeal Wheat Treats

For more natural sweetness, add 2 ounces (50g) raisins when stirring in the nuts.

2½ ounces (60g) plain flour
2½ ounces (60g) whole wheat flour
¼ teaspoon bicarbonate of soda
2 ounces (50g) butter *or* margarine
2 ounces (50g) lard
2 ounces (50g) caster sugar
2 ounces (50g) soft brown sugar
1 egg
2 tablespoons milk
1 or 2 drops vanilla essence
3 ounces (75g) quick-cooking rolled oats
1 ounce (25g) chopped walnuts

Lightly grease a baking tray. Set aside. In a small mixing bowl stir together plain flour, whole wheat flour, and soda (see photo 1, page 14). Set aside.

In a large mixing bowl beat butter or margarine and lard with an electric mixer on medium speed for 30 seconds. Add caster sugar and brown sugar and beat until fluffy (see photo 1, page 31). Add egg, milk, and vanilla essence and beat well. Gradually add flour mixture, beating until combined. Stir in oats and nuts.

Drop by rounded teaspoons 2 inches (5cm) apart onto the prepared baking tray (see photo 2, page 31). Bake in a 375°F (190°C) gas mark 5 oven about 10 minutes or until bottoms are lightly browned (see photo 3, page 31). Cool on baking tray for 1 minute. Remove and cool completely on wire racks (see photo 4, page 31). Makes about 36.

Hazelnut-Mocha Marvels

1 ounce (25g) plain flour
1 teaspoon ground cinnamon
¼ teaspoon baking powder
12 ounces (350g) plain chocolate pieces
2 ounces (50g) unsweetened chocolate
2 tablespoons instant coffee crystals
2 tablespoons butter *or* margarine
2 eggs
4 ounces (110g) soft brown sugar
2 or 3 drops vanilla essence
4 ounces (110g) chopped hazelnuts *or* walnuts

Lightly grease a baking tray. Set aside. In a mixing bowl combine flour, cinnamon, and baking powder (see photo 1, page 14). Set aside.

In a medium heavy saucepan heat *6 ounces* (175g) of the chocolate pieces, unsweetened chocolate, coffee crystals, and butter or margarine over low heat until melted, stirring constantly. Transfer to a small mixing bowl and cool slightly.

Add eggs, brown sugar, and vanilla essence to chocolate mixture and beat well. Gradually add flour mixture, beating until combined. Stir in remaining chocolate pieces and nuts.

Drop by heaping teaspoons 2 inches (5cm) apart onto the prepared baking tray (see photo 2, page 31). Bake in a 350°F (180°C) gas mark 4 oven for 8 to 10 minutes or until a slight finger imprint remains (see photo 3, page 31). Cool on baking tray for 1 minute. Remove and cool completely on wire racks (see photo 4, page 31). Makes about 30.

Coconut-Almond Marvels: Prepare Hazelnut-Mocha Marvels as above, *except* omit cinnamon, coffee crystals, and nuts. Stir 1½ ounces (40g) *coconut* and 2 ounces (50g) slivered *almonds,* toasted, into the dough.

Soured Cream Apricot Drops

Because there's soured cream in both the dough and the icing, store these Apricot Drops in the refrigerator.

5 **ounces (150g) plain flour**
4 **ounces (110g) whole wheat flour**
1 **teaspoon baking powder**
¼ **teaspoon bicarbonate of soda**
¼ **teaspoon ground allspice**
⅛ **teaspoon ground ginger**
4 **ounces (110g) butter *or* margarine**
3 **ounces (75g) caster sugar**
3 **ounces (75g) soft brown sugar**
1 **egg**
1 **or 2 drops vanilla essence**
4 **ounces (75g) dairy soured cream**
6 **ounces (175g) dried apricots, snipped**
   Soured Cream Icing

Lightly grease a baking tray. Set aside. In a medium mixing bowl stir together flours, baking powder, soda, allspice, and ginger (see photo 1, page 14). Set aside.

In a large mixing bowl beat butter or margarine with an electric mixer on medium speed for 30 seconds. Add caster sugar and brown sugar; beat until fluffy (see photo 1, page 31). Add egg and vanilla essence and beat well. Gradually add flour mixture and soured cream alternately to beaten mixture, beating well after each addition. Stir in apricots.

Drop by rounded teaspoons 2 inches (5cm) apart onto the prepared baking tray (see photo 2, page 31). Bake in a 350°F (180°C) gas mark 4 oven for 10 to 12 minutes or until bottoms are lightly browned (see photo 3, page 31). Cool on baking tray for 1 minute. Remove and cool completely on wire racks (see photo 4, page 31). Ice Apricot Drops with Soured Cream Icing. Makes about 42.

Soured Cream Icing: In a medium mixing bowl combine 2 ounces (50g) *soured cream;* 2 tablespoons *butter or margarine,* softened; and 1 or 2 drops *vanilla essence.* Gradually beat in 8 ounces (225g) sifted *icing sugar.* If necessary, add additional *icing sugar* to make spreadable.

Rough and Ready Ranger Biscuits

6 **ounces (175g) plain flour**
½ **teaspoon bicarbonate of soda**
¼ **teaspoon ground allspice**
4 **ounces (110g) butter *or* margarine**
4 **ounces (110g) soft brown sugar**
2 **ounces (50g) caster sugar**
1 **egg**
2 **or 3 drops vanilla essence**
1 **ounce (25g) wheat flakes**
1½ **ounces (40g) coconut**
4½ **ounces (125g) chopped peanuts**

In a mixing bowl stir together flour, soda, and allspice (see photo 1, page 14). Set aside.

In a large mixing bowl beat butter or margarine with an electric mixer on medium speed for 30 seconds. Add brown sugar and caster sugar and beat until fluffy (see photo 1, page 31). Add egg and vanilla essence and beat well. Gradually add flour mixture, beating until combined. Stir in wheat flakes, coconut, and peanuts.

Drop by rounded teaspoons 2 inches (5cm) apart onto an ungreased baking tray (see photo 2, page 31). Bake in a 375°F (190°C) gas mark 5 oven for 8 to 10 minutes or until bottoms are lightly browned (see photo 3, page 31). Cool on baking tray for 1 minute. Remove and cool completely on wire racks (see photo 4, page 31). Makes about 48.

◀ *Pictured opposite: Soured Cream Apricot Drops*

Monster Mouthfuls

Fee, fi, fo, fum, we smell a delicious cookie and we want one!

The next time you hear clamours for a super-duper treat, bake a fruity Ambrosia Cookie Pizza or a chewy Big Chipper Cookiewich.

Giant in both size and flavour, these monstrous cookies are a mouthful. Yet, even the most timid cook won't be scared off by these colossal cookies, because they're a snap to make.

Ambrosia Cookie Pizza

Ambrosia Cookie Pizza

Pizza party takes on a whole new meaning with this colourful dessert treat!

4 **ounces (110g) butter *or* margarine**
2 **ounces (50g) caster sugar**
2 **ounces (50g) soft brown sugar**
1 **egg**
½ **teaspoon finely grated orange peel**
2 **tablespoons orange juice**
7½ **ounces (210g) plain flour**
3 **ounces (75g) cream cheese, softened**
1 **egg**
3 **ounces (75g) orange marmalade**
2 **ounces (50g) sliced almonds, toasted**
1 **ounce (25g) desiccated coconut, toasted**
2 **ounces (50g) diced glacé peel (orange)**
Glacé cherries, sliced (optional)
Glacé pineapple, halved (optional)

Lightly grease a 12-inch (30cm) pizza tin. Set aside. For crust, in a large mixing bowl beat butter or margarine with an electric mixer on medium speed for 30 seconds. Add caster sugar and brown sugar and beat until fluffy (see photo 1, page 31). Add 1 egg, orange peel, and orange juice; beat well. Gradually add flour, beating until combined.

Spread crust mixture evenly into prepared tin (see photo 1). Bake in a 375°F (190°C) gas mark 5 oven about 18 minutes or until golden brown.

Meanwhile, in a small mixing bowl beat together cream cheese, 1 egg, and orange marmalade (mixture will be thin). Spread cream cheese mixture evenly over hot crust to within ½ inch (1cm) of edges (see photo 2). Sprinkle almonds, coconut, and glacé peel over the top (see photo 3). Garnish with glacé cherries and glacé pineapple, if desired. Return cookie pizza to the oven and bake for 5 minutes more.

Cool completely in tin on a wire rack. Cut into wedges (see photo 4). Makes 16 servings.

1 Use a rubber scraper or a knife to spread the batter into a greased 12-inch (30cm) pizza tin. As with bars, spread the batter evenly so you'll have an evenly baked crust.

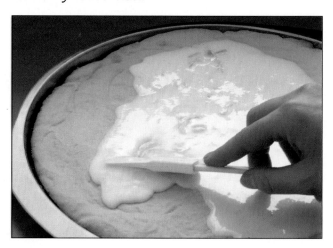

2 Spread the cream cheese mixture over baked crust to within ½ inch (1cm) of the edges. The mixture will be thin, so spread it carefully.

3 Scatter toasted almonds and coconut and glacé orange peel over the cream cheese mixture. For more colour, add glacé cherries and glacé pineapple slices, too.

4 Leave the cookie pizza in the tin and cool it completely on a wire rack. To serve, cut it into wedges with a sharp knife.

Big Chipper Cookiewich

6	ounces (175g) plain flour
1	teaspoon baking powder
¼	teaspoon bicarbonate of soda
2	ounces (50g) butter *or* margarine
2	ounces (50g) lard
3	ounces (75g) soft brown sugar
1½	ounces (40g) caster sugar
1	egg
2	or 3 drops vanilla essence
6	ounces (175g) miniature plain chocolate pieces *or* chocolate drops
4	ounces (110g) frozen whipped dessert topping, thawed

Lightly grease two 9x1½-inch (23x4cm) round baking tins. Set aside. In a medium mixing bowl stir together flour, baking powder, and soda (see photo 1, page 14). Set aside.

In a large mixing bowl beat butter or margarine and lard with an electric mixer on medium speed for 30 seconds. Add brown sugar and caster sugar and beat until fluffy (see photo 1, page 31). Add egg and vanilla essence and beat well. Gradually add flour mixture, beating until combined. Stir in chocolate pieces.

Divide dough in half. Spread each half into one of the prepared baking tins (see photo 1). Bake in a 350°F (180°C) gas mark 4 oven for 15 to 17 minutes or until golden. Cool in baking tins for 5 minutes. Remove and cool completely on wire racks.

To assemble, place 1 cookie on a flat plate, bottom side up. Spread thawed dessert topping over the cookie. Carefully top with the second cookie, bottom side down. Cover tightly with foil. Chill several hours or overnight. Cut into wedges (see photo 4). Makes 16 servings.

Specially Hand-Shaped

Hocus, pocus, mix it up—
from plain dough to special
cut-ups. A little magic
transforms every biscuit
dough into a one-of-a-kind
creation.

   Each biscuit is shaped by
hand, so it's extra-special. A
little time and care is all it
takes to make these
magical munchies.

   Watch out though!
These hand-crafted
biscuits might disappear
before your very eyes.

Peanut Butter Animals

Peanut Butter Animals

9	**ounces (250g) plain flour**
2½	**ounces (60g) whole wheat flour**
1½	**teaspoons bicarbonate of soda**
9	**ounces (250g) peanut butter**
4	**ounces (110g) butter *or* margarine**
4	**ounces (110g) lard**
9	**ounces (250g) caster sugar**
3	**ounces (75g) soft brown sugar**
2	**eggs**
2	**or 3 drops vanilla *essence***
	Miniature plain chocolate pieces *or* chocolate drops
	Decorating Icing (optional)

In a medium mixing bowl combine flours and soda (see photo 1, page 14). Set aside.

In large mixing bowl beat peanut butter, butter or margarine, and lard with electric mixer for 30 seconds. Add sugar and brown sugar; beat until fluffy (see photo 1, page 31). Add eggs and vanilla essence; beat well. Gradually stir or beat in flour mixture until combined (see photo 1).

Shape dough into balls and ropes (see photo 2). Arrange on an ungreased baking tray to form desired shapes. Flatten dough slightly and press together. Lightly press chocolate pieces into each biscuit, creating eyes, buttons, or noses.

Bake in a 350°F (180°C) gas mark 4 oven for 10 to 12 minutes or until edges are firm and bottoms are lightly browned (see photo 3). Cool on baking tray for 1 minute. Remove and cool on wire racks (see photo 4, page 31). If desired, pipe on bow ties or aprons with Decorating Icing. Makes about 36 large biscuits.

Decorating Icing: Combine 2 ounces (50g) sifted *icing sugar* and enough *milk* (about 2 teaspoons) to make of piping consistency.

1 Work the dry ingredients into the beaten mixture in one of two ways. Simply stir the dry ingredients in with a wooden spoon or beat them in with an electric mixer.

If you're using a portable hand mixer, stir in the last half of the dry ingredients by hand. Otherwise, you risk burning out the mixer motor.

2 Shape the dough into ropes by rolling it on the counter. *Or,* roll the dough between your palms into different sizes of balls.

3 Bake the biscuits until the edges are firm and the bottoms are a light, golden brown (as shown). If the edges are doughy, bake the biscuits a bit longer.

Honey 'n' Spice Biscuits

9 ounces (250g) plain flour
¼ teaspoon bicarbonate of soda
¼ teaspoon cream of tartar
¼ teaspoon ground nutmeg
2 ounces (50g) butter *or* margarine
2 ounces (50g) lard
4 ounces (110g) caster sugar
1 egg
2 tablespoons honey
2 or 3 drops vanilla essence
2 tablespoons caster sugar
½ teaspoon ground cinnamon

In a small mixing bowl stir together flour, soda, cream of tartar, and nutmeg (see photo 1, page 14). Set aside.

In a large mixing bowl beat butter or margarine and lard with an electric mixer on medium speed for 30 seconds. Add the 4 ounces (110g) sugar and beat until fluffy (see photo 1, page 31). Add egg, honey, and vanilla essence and beat well. Gradually stir or beat in flour mixture until combined (see photo 1, page 42).

Shape dough into 1¼-inch (3cm) balls (see photo 2, page 43). In a pie plate or shallow bowl stir together the 2 tablespoons sugar and cinnamon. Roll balls in sugar-cinnamon mixture to coat. Place balls 2 inches (5cm) apart on an ungreased baking tray. Flatten slightly with the bottom of a glass.

Bake in a 375°F (190°C) gas mark 5 oven about 8 minutes or until edges are firm and bottoms are lightly browned (see photo 3, page 43). Remove and cool completely on wire racks (see photo 4, page 31). Makes about 36.

Whole Wheat-Peanut Butter Blossoms

5 ounces (150g) plain flour
4 ounces (110g) whole wheat flour
1 teaspoon baking powder
⅛ teaspoon bicarbonate of soda
4 ounces (110g) lard
4½ ounces (125g) peanut butter
3 ounces (75g) caster sugar
3 ounces (75g) soft brown sugar
1 egg
2 tablespoons milk
2 or 3 drops vanilla essence
3 ounces (75g) chopped peanuts
Caster sugar
Milk chocolate buttons *or* kisses

In a medium mixing bowl stir together flours, baking powder, and soda (see photo 1, page 14). Set aside.

In a large mixing bowl beat lard and peanut butter with an electric mixer on medium speed for 30 seconds. Add the 3 ounces (75g) caster sugar and brown sugar and beat until fluffy (see photo 1, page 31). Add egg, milk, and vanilla essence; beat well. Gradually stir or beat in flour mixture until combined (see photo 1, page 42). Stir in peanuts.

Shape dough into 1-inch (2.5cm) balls (see photo 2, page 43). Place additional caster sugar in a pie plate or shallow bowl. Roll balls in caster sugar to coat. Place balls 2 inches (5cm) apart on an ungreased baking tray.

Bake in a 350°F (180°C) gas mark 4 oven for 10 to 12 minutes or until edges are firm and bottoms are lightly browned (see photo 3, page 43). Immediately press a chocolate button into each biscuit. Remove and cool on wire racks (see photo 4, page 31). Makes about 54.

▶ *Pictured opposite: Whole Wheat-Peanut Butter Blossoms*

David —
Love + Kisses
Lynda

Praline Sandies

We loaded our variation of this rich, buttery, American holiday classic with lots and lots of chopped nuts.

8 ounces (225g) butter *or* margarine
2 ounces (50g) soft brown sugar
1 tablespoon rum
2 or 3 drops vanilla essence
11 ounces (300g) plain flour
5 ounces (150g) chopped walnuts *or* pecans
1 ounce (25g) sifted icing sugar

In a large mixing bowl beat butter or margarine with an electric mixer on medium speed for 30 seconds. Add brown sugar and beat until fluffy (see photo 1, page 31). Add rum and vanilla essence and beat well. Gradually stir or beat in flour and walnuts or pecans until combined (see photo 1, page 42).

Shape dough into 1-inch (2.5cm) balls or 1½x½-inch (4x1cm) ropes (see photo 2, page 43). Place 2 inches (5cm) apart on an ungreased baking tray.

Bake in a 325°F (170°C) gas mark 3 oven about 20 minutes or until edges are firm and bottoms are lightly browned (see photo 3, page 43). Remove and cool completely on wire racks (see photo 4, page 31). In a polythene bag gently shake a few at a time in icing sugar. Makes about 48.

Old-Fashioned Sandies: Prepare Praline Sandies as described above, *except* substitute *caster sugar* for the soft brown sugar, omit the rum, and use 2 teaspoons *water* and 4 or 5 drops *vanilla essence.*

Chocolate-Topped Almond Fingers

14 ounces (400g) plain flour
¼ teaspoon bicarbonate of soda
8 ounces (225g) butter *or* margarine
6 ounces (175g) caster sugar
1 egg
2 tablespoons milk
2 or 3 drops vanilla essence
2 ounces (50g) finely chopped almonds, toasted
2 ounces (50g) plain chocolate pieces
1 tablespoon lard
2 fluid ounces (55ml) Amaretto
4 to 4½ ounces (110 to 125g) sifted icing sugar
Finely chopped almonds, toasted (optional)

In a medium mixing bowl stir together flour and soda (see photo 1, page 14). Set aside.

In a large mixing bowl beat butter or margarine with an electric mixer on medium speed for 30 seconds. Add sugar and beat until fluffy (see photo 1, page 31). Add egg, milk, and vanilla essence and beat well. Gradually stir or beat in flour mixture until combined (see photo 1, page 42). Stir in the 2 ounces (50g) almonds. If necessary, cover and chill about 1 hour or until easy to handle.

Roll rounded teaspoons of dough into 2-inch (5cm) ropes (see photo 2, page 43). Place ropes 1½ inches (4cm) apart on an ungreased baking tray. Bake in a 375°F (190°C) gas mark 5 oven for 6 to 8 minutes or until edges are firm and bottoms are lightly browned (see photo 3, page 43). Remove and cool completely on wire racks (see photo 4, page 31).

In a small heavy saucepan melt chocolate and lard over low heat, stirring constantly. Stir in Amaretto and enough icing sugar to make of drizzling consistency. Drizzle melted chocolate mixture over Almond Fingers. (If mixture thickens while drizzling, stir in hot *water,* a few drops at a time.) Sprinkle with additional finely chopped almonds, if desired. Makes about 60.

Black Treacle-Spice Biscuits

You'll be amazed how fast these spicy, chewy treats disappear.

11 ounces (300g) plain flour
2 teaspoons bicarbonate of soda
1 teaspoon ground ginger
½ teaspoon ground allspice *or* ground cinnamon
¼ teaspoon ground mace *or* ground cloves
6 ounces (175g) lard
6 ounces (175g) soft brown sugar
1 egg
2 fluid ounces (55ml) black treacle
1 teaspoon finely grated lemon peel (optional)
   Caster sugar

In a large mixing bowl stir together flour, soda, ginger, allspice or cinnamon, and mace or cloves (see photo 1, page 14). Set aside.

In a large mixing bowl beat lard with an electric mixer on medium speed for 30 seconds. Add brown sugar and beat until fluffy (see photo 1, page 31). Add the egg, treacle, and lemon peel, if desired, and beat well. Gradually stir or beat in the flour mixture until combined (see photo 1, page 42).

Shape dough into 1¼-inch (3cm) balls (see photo 2, page 43). Place caster sugar in a pie plate or shallow bowl. Roll balls in sugar to coat. Place balls 2 inches (5cm) apart on an ungreased baking tray.

Bake in a 375°F (190°C) gas mark 5 oven for 8 to 10 minutes or until edges are firm and bottoms are lightly browned (see photo 3, page 43). Cool on baking tray for 1 minute. Remove and cool completely on wire racks (see photo 4, page 31). Makes about 48.

Peppered Pfeffernuesse

Saying Peppered Pfeffernuesse (FEF-uhr-noos) is fun, but not as much fun as eating these spicy German Christmas cookies that typically contain pepper.

3 fluid ounces (80ml) black treacle
2 ounces (50g) butter *or* margarine
10 ounces (275g) plain flour
1½ ounces (40g) soft brown sugar
¾ teaspoon ground cinnamon
½ teaspoon bicarbonate of soda
½ teaspoon aniseed, crushed
¼ teaspoon ground cardamom
¼ teaspoon ground allspice
   Dash pepper
1 beaten egg
2 tablespoons finely chopped glace peel (optional)
   Sifted icing sugar

In a large saucepan combine treacle and butter or margarine. Heat and stir over low heat until butter or margarine melts. Remove from heat. Cool to room temperature.

Meanwhile, in a large mixing bowl stir together flour, brown sugar, cinnamon, soda, aniseed, cardamom, allspice, and pepper (see photo 1, page 14). Set aside.

Stir egg into cooled treacle mixture. Gradually stir in flour mixture until combined (see photo 1, page 42). Stir in glace peel, if desired. If necessary, transfer dough to a bowl and cover and chill about 1 hour or until easy to handle.

Grease a baking tray. Set aside. Shape dough into 1¼-inch (3cm) balls (see photo 2, page 43). Place 1 inch (2.5cm) apart on prepared baking tray. Bake in a 350°F (180°C) gas mark 4 oven for 10 to 12 minutes or until edges are firm and bottoms are lightly browned (see photo 3, page 43). Remove and cool completely on wire racks (see photo 4, page 31). Roll in icing sugar to coat. Makes about 36.

Make-a-Biscuit Mix

The next time you want to give your kids a special treat, have a batch of biscuits waiting. It's fast and easy with our homemade mix.

These biscuits start with a basic mix you can keep on hand for months.

Choose Cranberry Drops, Great Cocoa Bars, or decorative American Gumdrop Biscuits. No matter which recipe you pick, you're sure to please every child in the neighbourhood.

American Gumdrop Biscuits

Make-a-Biscuit Mix

Store this handy homemade mix in the freezer for 6 months or in the refrigerator for 6 weeks.

20 ounces (560g) plain flour
6 ounces (175g) caster sugar
6 ounces (175g) soft brown sugar
2 teaspoons baking powder
12 ounces lard

In a large mixing bowl stir together flour, sugar, brown sugar, and baking powder (see photo 1, page 14). Cut in lard until mixture resembles fine crumbs (see photo 1). Store tightly covered in the refrigerator for up to 6 weeks.

To measure, weigh mix or spoon it into a measure and level with a spatula (see photo 2). Makes about 44 ounces (1kg250g).

1 Use a pastry blender or fork to work the lard into the flour mixture till it's cut up into fine crumbs, as shown.

American Gumdrop Biscuits

3 ounces (75g) American hard gumdrops
16 ounces (450g) Make-a-Biscuit Mix
1 slightly beaten egg
2 or 3 drops vanilla essence
Caster sugar
Hard gumdrops (optional)

Finely chop the gumdrops (see photo 3). In a large mixing bowl stir together gumdrops, Make-a-Biscuit Mix, egg, and vanilla essence. Shape dough into 1½-inch (4cm) balls (see photo 2, page 43). Place balls 2 inches (5cm) apart on an ungreased baking tray. Flatten slightly with the bottom of a glass dipped in caster sugar. Cut decorative shapes from additional gumdrops and press lightly into biscuits, if desired.

Bake in a 375°F (190°C) gas mark 5 oven for 8 to 10 minutes or until bottoms are lightly browned (see photo 3, page 43). Remove and cool completely on wire racks (see photo 4, page 31). Makes about 24.

2 To measure dry ingredients such as the Make-a-Biscuit Mix, weigh accurately or use a measure exactly the size you need. Spoon the mix lightly into the jug, then level it off with a metal spatula or the flat side of a knife.

3 On a cutting board, use a sharp knife to finely chop the gumdrops. If the knife gets sticky, dip the blade into cold water. *Or,* try snipping the gumdrops into small pieces with kitchen scissors.

Great Cocoa Bars

Moist and mouth-watering, these quick-to-fix bars make an irresistible chocolate treat.

14 ounces (400g) Make-a-Biscuit Mix
1½ ounces (40g) caster sugar
1 ounce (25g) unsweetened cocoa powder
1 slightly beaten egg
4 fluid ounces (110ml) milk
3 ounces (75g) plain chocolate, chopped into small pieces
2½ ounces (60g) chopped nuts
Icing sugar

Grease a 9x9x2-inch (23x23x5cm) baking tin. Set aside. In a large mixing bowl stir together Make-a-Biscuit Mix, sugar, and cocoa powder. In a small mixing bowl stir together egg and milk. Stir into dry ingredients, along with chocolate pieces and nuts. Spread batter evenly into prepared tin (see photo 3, page 15).

Bake in a 350°F (180°C) gas mark 4 oven for 25 to 30 minutes or until a wooden toothpick inserted in centre comes out clean (see photo 4, page 15). Cool completely on a wire rack. Sift icing sugar over top. Cut into bars (see photo 5, page 15). Makes 24.

Raisin Bars

15 ounces (425g) Make-a-Biscuit Mix
5 ounces (150g) raisins
3 ounces (75g) apple puree
2 slightly beaten eggs
1 tablespoon milk
2 or 3 drops vanilla essence
¼ teaspoon ground cinnamon
¼ teaspoon ground nutmeg
Spice Icing
Ground nutmeg

Grease a 9x9x2-inch (23x23x5cm) baking tin. Set aside. In a medium mixing bowl stir Make-a-Biscuit Mix, raisins, apple puree, eggs, milk, vanilla, cinnamon, and nutmeg. Mix well.

Spread batter evenly into prepared tin (see photo 3, page 15). Bake in a 350°F (180°C) gas mark 4 oven about 25 minutes or until a wooden toothpick inserted in centre comes out clean (see photo 4, page 15). Cool completely on a wire rack. Spread with Spice Icing. Sprinkle with nutmeg. Cut into bars (see photo 5, page 15). Makes 36.

Spice Icing: In a small mixing bowl beat together 6 ounces (175g) sifted *icing sugar;* 3 tablespoons *butter or margarine,* softened; and ¼ teaspoon ground *cinnamon.* Add enough *milk* (1 to 2 tablespoons) to make spreadable.

◀ *Pictured opposite: Raisin Bars*

Cranberry Drops

16   ounces (450g) Make-a-Biscuit Mix
½   teaspoon ground nutmeg
1   slightly beaten egg
2   tablespoons orange juice
6   ounces (175g) finely chopped
     cranberries (8 ounces [225g]
     unchopped)
2½ ounces (60g) chopped walnuts

In a large mixing bowl stir together Make-a-Biscuit Mix and nutmeg. Stir in egg and orange juice. Mix well. Stir in cranberries and nuts.

Drop by rounded teaspoons 2 inches (5cm) apart onto an ungreased baking tray (see photo 2, page 31). Bake in a 350°F (180°C) gas mark 4 oven about 20 minutes or until bottoms are lightly browned (see photo 3, page 31). Remove and cool completely on wire racks (see photo 4, page 31). Makes about 42.

Oatmeal-Peanut Biscuits

14   ounces (400g) Make-a-Biscuit Mix
1½ ounces (40g) soft brown sugar
2   slightly beaten eggs
4   fluid ounces (110ml) milk
1   or 2 drops vanilla essence
3   ounces (75g) quick-cooking rolled oats
5   ounces (150g) chopped peanuts

In a large mixing bowl stir together Make-a-Biscuit Mix, brown sugar, eggs, milk, and vanilla essence. Mix well. Stir in oats and peanuts.

Drop by rounded teaspoons 2 inches (5cm) apart onto an ungreased baking tray (see photo 2, page 31). Bake in a 375°F (190°C) gas mark 5 oven for 8 to 10 minutes or till bottoms are lightly browned (see photo 3, page 31). Remove and cool completely on wire racks (see photo 4, page 31). Makes about 42.

All About Baking Trays

Baking trays are more than just sheets that hold dollops of cookie or biscuit dough. They affect the colour, shape, and texture of your baked cookies or biscuits.
● When you're shopping for a baking tray, look for a shiny, heavy-gauge aluminium one with very low sides or no sides at all.
● Avoid dark baking trays because they absorb heat and may cause overbrowning on the bottoms of cookies. Nonstick baking trays work well if they're not too dark.
● Keep the size of your oven in mind, too: there should be 1 to 2 inches (2.5 to 5cm) between the tray and the oven walls and door to allow for good air circulation. And even if your oven is small, don't put one tray directly over another one. This also results in poor air circulation within the oven.
● Grease baking trays only when the recipe recommends it. Otherwise, cookies may spread too much.
● Nonstick trays sometimes cause a slight variance in cookie texture. Because liquids bead up on nonstick surfaces, the cookie batter doesn't spread quite as much. The baked results are a little thicker, with very smooth bottoms.

Banana Chippers

Keep these chippers in the freezer to store them longer than one day.

16   **ounces (450g) Make-a-Biscuit Mix**
  4   **ounces (110g) mashed banana**
  1   **slightly beaten egg**
  1   **or 2 drops vanilla essence**
  3   **ounces (75g) miniature plain**
        chocolate pieces

In a large mixing bowl stir together Make-a-Biscuit Mix, banana, egg, and vanilla essence. Mix well. Stir in chocolate pieces.

Drop by rounded teaspoons 2 inches (5cm) apart onto an ungreased baking tray (see photo 2, page 31). Bake in a 375°F (190°C) gas mark 5 oven about 10 minutes or until bottoms are lightly browned (see photo 3, page 31). Remove and cool completely on wire racks (see photo 4, page 31). Makes about 36.

Carrot Drops

How can you make these soft carrot drops even better? Top them with the Cream Cheese Icing on page 17.

14   **ounces (400g) Make-a-Biscuit Mix**
  5   **ounces (150g) finely grated carrot**
  1   **ounce (25g) toasted wheat germ**
  ½   **teaspoon finely grated orange peel**
  1   **slightly beaten egg**
  2   **tablespoons milk**
  1   **or 2 drops vanilla essence**

Mix Make-a-Biscuit Mix, carrot, wheat germ, and orange peel. Combine egg, milk, and vanilla essence. Stir into carrot mixture, mixing well.

Drop by rounded teaspoons 2 inches (5cm) apart onto an ungreased baking tray (see photo 2, page 31). Bake in a 375°F (190°C) gas mark 4 oven for 8 to 10 minutes or until bottoms are lightly browned (see photo 3, page 31). Remove and cool completely on wire racks (see photo 4, page 31). Makes about 30.

Jam Gems

These yummy Jam Gems puff high as they bake and flatten out again as they cool.

11   **ounces (300g) Make-a-Biscuit Mix**
  1   **slightly beaten egg yolk**
  2   **tablespoons milk**
  1   **teaspoon finely grated lemon peel**
  2   **or 3 drops vanilla essence**
  1   **slightly beaten egg white**
3½   **ounces (85g) finely chopped walnuts**
        ***or* pecans**
  2   **tablespoons desired jam**

Grease a baking tray. Set aside. In a medium mixing bowl stir together Make-a-Biscuit Mix, egg yolk, milk, lemon peel, and vanilla essence. Cover and chill about 30 minutes or until mixture is easy to handle.

Shape dough into 1¼-inch (3cm) balls (see photo 2, page 43). Roll each ball in the beaten egg white, then in the nuts. Place 2 inches (5cm) apart on prepared baking tray. Press down centres with a moistened finger.

Bake in a 350°F (180°C) gas mark 4 oven for 14 to 15 minutes or until bottoms are lightly browned (see photo 3, page 43). Remove and cool completely on wire racks (see photo 4, page 31). Spoon about *¼ teaspoon* jam into the centre of *each* Jam Gem. Store overnight in the refrigerator or freeze for longer storage. Makes about 24.

Roped Delights

At the end of your rope trying to decide what kind of cookie or biscuit to make? We've got the answer to your dilemma.

Citrus Kringla or Cinnamon Candy Cane Cookies will add a new twist to any cookie or biscuit jar.

Meander through this chapter and enjoy every cookie and biscuit. One nibble and you'll be roped into baking these cookies and biscuits for family and friends.

Spicy Wheat Wreaths

Spicy Wheat Wreaths

5	**ounces (150g) plain flour**
¼	**teaspoon baking powder**
2½	**ounces (60g) whole wheat flour**
½	**teaspoon ground cinnamon**
¼	**teaspoon ground ginger**
	Dash ground cloves
6	**ounces (175g) butter or margarine**
4½	**ounces (125g) caster sugar**
1	**egg**
2	**or 3 drops vanilla essence**
2½	**ounces (60g) plain flour**
12	**red or green glacé cherries, halved**

Combine the 5 ounces (150g) plain flour and baking powder (see photo 1, page 14). Set aside. Combine whole wheat flour, cinnamon, ginger, and cloves (see photo 1, page 14). Set aside.

In a large mixing bowl beat butter or margarine with an electric mixer on medium speed for 30 seconds. Add sugar and beat until fluffy (see photo 1, page 31). Add egg and vanilla essence; beat well. Gradually add flour-baking powder mixture, beating until combined. Divide dough in half.

Add whole wheat flour mixture to one half, stirring until combined. Add the 2½ ounces (60g) plain flour to the other half, stirring until combined. Cover each half and chill about 30 minutes or until easy to handle.

On a lightly floured surface roll *each* half into a 12-inch (30cm) log (see photo 1). Cut *each* log into *twenty-four* ½-inch (about 1cm) pieces (see photo 2). Roll each piece into a 6-inch (15cm) rope. Place a white and a brown rope side by side and twist together about 6 times (see photo 3). Shape twisted ropes into a circle, gently pinching where ends meet (see photo 4). Place 2 inches (5cm) apart on an ungreased baking tray. Place *1* cherry half over the spot where the ends meet on *each* wreath.

Bake in a 375°F (190°C) gas mark 5 oven for 8 to 10 minutes or until edges are firm (see photo 3, page 43). Cool on baking tray for 1 minute. Remove and cool (see photo 4, page 31). Makes 24.

1 Shape the dough into a log by working it with your hands and rolling it on a lightly floured counter till it measures the correct length. Lay a ruler down next to the log so the size is easy to check.

2 Using a sharp, thin-bladed knife, cut the log into the correct number of pieces. Use the ruler again to make sure each piece is the size called for in the recipe.

3 Roll each small piece of dough into a thin rope. Place a white rope and a brown rope side by side and twist several times.

4 Bring the two rope ends together to form a circle. Gently pinch the ends together where they meet.

Citrus Kringla

The soft dough of these Norwegian favourites bakes into a tender, cake-like cookie.

15   ounces (425g) plain flour
2½   teaspoons baking powder
1   teaspoon bicarbonate of soda
4   ounces (110g) butter *or* margarine
6   ounces (175g) caster sugar
1   egg
1½   teaspoons finely grated lemon peel *or* orange peel
6   fluid ounces (165ml) buttermilk

In a medium mixing bowl stir together flour, baking powder, and soda (see photo 1, page 14). Set aside.

In a large mixing bowl beat butter or margarine with an electric mixer on medium speed for 30 seconds. Add sugar and beat until fluffy (see photo 1, page 31). Add egg and lemon peel or orange peel and beat well. Add flour mixture and buttermilk alternately to beaten mixture, beating until combined. Cover and chill for 4 hours or overnight or until easy to handle.

Divide dough in half. (Return one half to the refrigerator until you're ready to work with it.) On a lightly floured surface roll each half into a 10x5-inch (25.5x13cm) rectangle. Cut each rectangle crosswise into twenty 5x½-inch (about 13x1cm) strips. Roll each strip into a 10-inch (25.5cm) rope (see photo 3, page 59).

On an ungreased baking tray shape each rope into a loop, crossing 1½ inches (4cm) from ends. Twist rope at crossing point. Lift ends over to top of loop and seal, forming a pretzel shape.

Bake in a 425°F (220°C) gas mark 7 oven about 5 minutes or until edges are firm and bottoms are lightly browned, though tops will be pale (see photo 3, page 43). Remove and cool completely on wire racks (see photo 4, page 31). Makes 40.

Cinnamon Candy Cane Biscuits

Cover the dough you're not working with and place it in the refrigerator so it doesn't dry out.

9   ounces (250g) plain flour
½   teaspoon baking powder
3   ounces (75g) lard
3   ounces (75g) butter *or* margarine
4   ounces (110g) caster sugar
1   egg
2   or 3 drops vanilla essence
2   drops oil of cinnamon *or* ½ teaspoon ground cinnamon
4   to 6 drops red food colouring

In a small bowl stir together flour and baking powder (see photo 1, page 14). Set aside.

In a large mixing bowl beat lard and butter or margarine with an electric mixer on medium speed for 30 seconds. Add sugar and beat until fluffy (see photo 1, page 31). Add egg, vanilla essence, and oil of cinnamon and beat well. Gradually add flour mixture, beating until combined. Divide dough in half. Stir food colouring into one half. Cover each half and chill about 30 minutes or until easy to handle.

Divide each colour of dough in half. On a lightly floured surface roll each portion of dough into a 9-inch (23cm) log (see photo 1, page 58). Cut *each* log into *eighteen* ½-inch (about 1cm) pieces (see photo 2, page 58). Roll each piece into a 4-inch (10cm) rope. Place a red and a white rope side by side and twist together (see photo 3, page 59). Pinch ends to seal (see photo 4, page 59). Form twisted ropes into a cane. Place 2 inches (5cm) apart on an ungreased baking tray.

Bake in a 375°F (190°C) gas mark 5 oven for 8 to 10 minutes or until edges are firm and bottoms are lightly browned (see photo 3, page 43). Remove and cool completely on wire racks (see photo 4, page 31). Makes 36.

Flaky Dutch Letters

10 **ounces (275g) almonds, finely ground**
2½ **ounces (60g) sifted icing sugar**
2 **egg whites**
2 **or 3 drops vanilla essence**
12 **ounces (350g) butter *or* margarine**
15 **ounces (425g) plain flour**
2 **fluid ounces (55ml) iced water**
1 **egg yolk**

For filling, in a small mixer bowl beat together ground almonds, icing sugar, egg whites, and vanilla essence. Cover and chill thoroughly.

For dough, in a large mixing bowl cut butter or margarine into flour until mixture resembles coarse crumbs (see photo 1, page 50). Sprinkle *1 tablespoon* iced water over part of mixture. Gently toss with fork and push to the side of the bowl. Repeat with remaining iced water until all is moistened. Form into a ball. Cover and let stand about 10 minutes or until easy to handle.

On a lightly floured surface roll dough into a 10x12-inch (25.5x30cm) rectangle. Fold into thirds. Repeat rolling and folding twice. Divide dough into thirds. Cover and set aside. With moistened hands, roll the filling into two 7½-inch (19cm) logs (see photo 1, page 58). Cut logs into 1-inch (2.5cm) pieces (see photo 2, page 58), combining the two ½-inch (1cm) pieces from the ends of both logs. Roll each piece of filling into a 7½-inch (19cm) rope (see photo 3, page 59). You'll have a total of 15.

On a lightly floured surface roll each third of dough into an 8x10-inch (20x25.5cm) rectangle. Cut into five 8x2-inch (20x5cm) strips. Place 1 filling rope on each strip of dough. Wrap dough around filling. Seal edges and ends. Shape into "S" shapes. Place 2 inches (5cm) apart on an ungreased baking tray.

In a small mixing bowl combine egg yolk and 1 tablespoon *water*. Brush on letters. Bake in a 375°F (190°C) gas mark 5 oven for 30 to 35 minutes or until golden. Remove and cool completely on wire racks (see photo 4, page 31). To store for more than 1 day, wrap and freeze. Makes 15.

Decorated Berliner Kranzer

These buttery, wreath-shaped Scandinavian favourites literally melt in your mouth.

8 **ounces (225g) butter *or* margarine**
2 **ounces (50g) sifted icing sugar**
1 **hard-boiled egg yolk, sieved**
1 **raw egg yolk**
¼ **teaspoon almond extract**
11 **ounces (300g) plain flour**
1 **slightly beaten egg white**
6 **to 8 sugar cubes, crushed**
Chopped red *or* green glacé cherries (optional)

In a large mixing bowl beat butter or margarine with an electric mixer on medium speed for 30 seconds. Add icing sugar and beat until fluffy (see photo 1, page 31). Add both egg yolks and almond extract and beat well. Gradually stir in flour until combined. Cover and chill about 1 hour or until easy to handle.

Divide dough in half. Roll each half into a 9-inch (23cm) log (see photo 1, page 58). Cut *each* log into *eighteen* ½-inch (about 1cm) pieces (see photo 2, page 58). Roll each piece into a 6-inch (15cm) rope (see photo 3, page 59). Shape each rope into a ring, overlapping about 1 inch (2.5cm) from ends. Brush with egg white and sprinkle with crushed sugar cubes. If desired, press a few pieces of chopped glacé cherries into the cookie at the point where the ropes overlap. Place 2 inches (5cm) apart on an ungreased baking tray.

Bake in a 350°F (180°C) gas mark 4 oven about 10 minutes or until edges are firm and bottoms are lightly browned (see photo 3, page 43). Remove and cool completely on wire racks (see photo 4, page 31). Makes 36.

Tasty Biscuit Tarts

Here's our candidate for "Biscuit Most Likely To Succeed"—whether it's for teatime or lunchtime or for family or guests.

Each rich, flaky pastry shell is not only a biscuit base, but also a delightful, edible container for a delectable filling.

So next time you vote for best biscuit, cast your ballot for these tiny biscuit tarts. They're a winner in every category.

Mini Cheesecake Tarts

Mini Cheesecake Tarts

Keep these melt-in-your-mouth morsels on hand in your freezer—they're ideal for spur-of-the-moment entertaining. Dollop each with jam just before serving.

5 ounces (150g) plain flour
2 ounces (50g) caster sugar
1 ounce (25g) unsweetened cocoa powder
4 ounces (110g) butter *or* margarine
2 to 3 tablespoons water
6 ounces (175g) cream cheese, softened
1½ ounces (40g) caster sugar
2 tablespoons milk
2 or 3 drops vanilla essence
1 egg
Jam *or* marmalade (optional)

For pastry, in a small mixing bowl stir together flour, the 2 ounces (50g) sugar, and cocoa powder. Cut in butter or margarine until pieces are the size of small peas (see photo 2, page 22). Sprinkle with water, 1 tablespoon at a time, tossing gently until all is moistened (photo 1).

Form dough into a ball. Divide dough into 24 balls. Place each ball in an ungreased 1¾-inch (4.5cm) deep patty tin. Press dough evenly against bottom and sides of tin (see photo 2).

For filling, in a small mixer bowl beat cream cheese and the 1½ ounces (40g) sugar until fluffy. Beat in milk and vanilla essence. Add egg and beat at low speed just until combined. Fill *each* pastry-lined patty tin with about *1 tablespoon* of the cream cheese filling (see photo 3).

Bake in a 325°F (170°C) gas mark 3 oven for 15 to 18 minutes or until done. Cool for 30 minutes in tins. Remove from tins and cool completely on wire racks (see photo 4). Top each tart with jam or marmalade, if desired. Makes 24.

1 Sprinkle 1 tablespoon water over part of the flour mixture. Gently toss with a fork. Push to the side of the bowl and repeat with remaining water till all of the mixture is moistened.

2 Press the dough *evenly* against the bottoms and sides of the patty tins. If the dough is too thin at any one place, the tarts may crack as they bake and allow the filling to leak through.

3 Use a measuring spoon to divide the filling mixture evenly among the patty tins.

4 It's easier to remove the tarts after baking if you let them cool slightly in the patty tins first. Then, carefully lift the tarts out with a metal spatula and let them finish cooling on wire racks.

Rocky Road Tarts

4 ounces (110g) butter *or* margarine,
   softened
3 ounces (75g) cream cheese, softened
5 ounces (150g) plain flour
1 ounce (25g) ground walnuts, pecans, *or*
   almonds
8 ounces (225g) milk chocolate, cut up
1½ ounces (40g) tiny marshmallows
2 ounces (50g) coarsely chopped
   walnuts, pecans, *or* almonds

For pastry, in a small mixing bowl beat together butter or margarine and cream cheese. Add flour and ground nuts, stirring until combined. Cover and chill dough about 1 hour or until easy to handle.

Divide dough into 24 balls. Place each ball in an ungreased 1¾-inch (4.5cm) deep patty tin. Press dough evenly against bottom and sides of tin (see photo 2, page 64). Bake in a 325°F (170°C) gas mark 3 oven for 20 to 22 minutes or until done. Cool slightly in tin.

Meanwhile, for filling, in a small heavy saucepan melt chocolate over low heat, stirring constantly. Remove saucepan from heat. Stir in marshmallows and chopped nuts.

Quickly fill *each* pastry-lined patty tin with about *1 rounded teaspoon* of filling (see photo 3, page 65). Chill until centre is firm. Remove from tins (see photo 4, page 65). Let stand at room temperature about 20 minutes before serving. Makes 24.

Fruited Sesame Tassies

Toasted sesame seed add a rich, nutty flavour to these bite-size titbits.

6 ounces (175g) mixed dried fruit
12 fluid ounces (330ml) water
5 ounces (150g) orange marmalade
1 tablespoon toasted sesame seed
4 ounces (110g) butter *or* margarine
1½ ounces (40g) soft brown sugar
2 tablespoons water
8 ounces (225g) plain flour
1 ounce (25g) quick-cooking rolled oats

For filling, in a small saucepan combine dried fruit and the 12 fluid ounces (330ml) water. Bring to boiling. Reduce heat and simmer, covered, for 8 minutes or until fruit is very tender. Drain. Stir marmalade and sesame seed into fruit. Set aside.

For pastry, in a small mixing bowl beat butter or margarine on medium speed of an electric mixer for 30 seconds. Add soft brown sugar and beat until fluffy (see photo 1, page 31). Beat in the 2 tablespoons water. Add flour and oats, stirring until combined.

Divide dough into 36 balls. Place each ball in an ungreased 1¾-inch (4.5cm) deep patty tin. Press dough evenly against bottom and sides of tin (see photo 2, page 64). Fill *each* pastry-lined patty tin with about *1 tablespoon* of the filling (see photo 3, page 65).

Bake in a 325°F (170°C) gas mark 3 oven for 28 to 30 minutes or until done. Cool for 5 minutes in tins. Remove from tins and cool completely on wire racks (see photo 4, page 65). Makes 36.

Fudgy Liqueur Cups

As one editor put it, "They're like eating fudge in a chocolate shell."

4   **ounces (110g) plain flour**
1   **ounce (25g) unsweetened cocoa
     powder**
3   **ounces (75g) butter *or* margarine,
     softened**
2   **ounces (50g) caster sugar**
3   **ounces (75g) cream cheese, softened**
4   **ounces (110g) butter *or* margarine**
3   **ounces (75g) caster sugar**
1½ **ounces (40g) unsweetened cocoa
     powder**
1   **egg**
2   **tablespoons Grand Marnier, Cointreau,
     or cherry liqueur**
2   **or 3 drops vanilla essence**

For pastry, in a small mixing bowl stir together flour and the 1 ounce (25g) cocoa powder. Set aside. In a small mixing bowl beat the 3 ounces (75g) butter or margarine, the 2 ounces (50g) sugar, and cream cheese until fluffy. Gradually add flour mixture, beating until combined. If necessary, cover and chill dough about 30 minutes or until easy to handle.

Divide dough into 24 balls. Place each ball in a lightly greased 1¾-inch (4.5cm) deep patty tin. Press dough evenly against bottom and sides of tin (see photo 2, page 64).

For filling, in a small saucepan melt the 4 ounces (110g) butter or margarine over low heat. Remove from heat and stir in the 3 ounces (75g) sugar; the 1½ ounce (40g) cocoa powder; egg; Grand Marnier, Cointreau, or cherry liqueur; and vanilla essence. Fill *each* pastry-lined patty tin with about *1 tablespoon* filling (see photo 3, page 65).

Bake in a 325°F (170°C) gas mark 3 oven about 18 minutes or until filling is set. Cool for 10 minutes in tins. Remove from tins and cool completely on wire racks (see photo 4, page 65). Makes 24.

Bonbon Bites

2   **ounces (50g) sweet plain chocolate**
3   **ounces (75g) butter *or* margarine,
     softened**
3   **ounces (75g) cream cheese, softened**
5   **ounces (150g) plain flour**
3   **ounces (75g) apricot preserves,
     seedless raspberry preserves, *or*
     cherry preserves**
½ **ounce (10g) plain chocolate**
1   **tablespoon butter *or* margarine**
2   **ounces (50g) sifted icing sugar**
1   **drop vanilla essence**
1   **tablespoon boiling water**

For pastry, in a small heavy saucepan melt 2 ounces (50g) sweet plain chocolate over low heat, stirring often. Remove saucepan from heat and cool slightly. In a small mixing bowl beat together the 3 ounces (75g) butter or margarine, cream cheese, and melted chocolate. Gradually add flour, beating until combined. Cover and chill dough about 1 hour or until easy to handle.

Divide dough into 24 balls. Place each ball in an ungreased 1¾-inch (4.5cm) deep patty tin. Press dough evenly against bottom and sides of tin (see photo 2, page 64).

Bake in a 350°F (180°C) gas mark 4 oven for 15 to 18 minutes or until done. Cool slightly in tins. Remove from tins and cool completely on wire racks (see photo 4, page 65). Fill *each* pastry-lined patty tin with about ½ *teaspoon* desired preserves (see photo 3, page 65).

In a small heavy saucepan melt plain chocolate and the 1 tablespoon butter or margarine over low heat, stirring often. Remove saucepan from heat and add icing sugar and vanilla essence; stirring until crumbly. Stir in water until smooth. (Add more *water,* a few drops at a time, if necessary, to make of drizzling consistency.) Drizzle a little of the chocolate mixture over each tart. Chill until chocolate drizzle is firm. Makes 24.

Biscuit Cut-outs

The sky's the limit! Let your imagination soar when you make a batch of these biscuit cut-outs.

One try at this biscuit-making method and you'll have earned your wings. Roll out the dough, then cut into shapes—any shape you like.

Our selection of high-in-the-sky flavours gives you everything you need to successfully land a crew of biscuit lovers.

High-in-the-Sky Biscuit Pops

High-in-the-Sky Biscuit Pops

14 **ounces (400g) plain flour**
1 **teaspoon bicarbonate of soda**
3 **ounces (75g) butter *or* margarine**
1½ **ounces (40g) caster sugar**
1 **egg**
6 **fluid ounces (165ml) honey**
½ **teaspoon lemon extract *or* 1 or 2 drops vanilla essence**
Wooden sticks
1 **egg yolk**
1 **teaspoon water**
Food colouring

In a medium mixing bowl stir together flour and soda (see photo 1, page 14). Set aside.

In a large mixing bowl beat butter or margarine with an electric mixer on medium speed for 30 seconds. Add caster sugar and beat until fluffy (see photo 1, page 31). Add egg, honey, and lemon extract or vanilla essence and beat well. Gradually add flour mixture, beating until combined. Divide biscuit dough into thirds. Cover and chill about 1 hour or until easy to handle. Meanwhile, cut moon, rainbow, and cloud shapes out of cardboard.

Grease a baking tray. Set aside. On a lightly floured surface roll dough ¼ inch (½cm) thick (see photo 1). Use a sharp knife to cut around cardboard patterns (see photo 2). For star shapes, use a biscuit cutter. Place 1 inch (2.5cm) apart on prepared baking tray. Tuck a wooden stick under the centre of each biscuit. Press dough around stick to secure (see photo 3).

In a small bowl beat together egg yolk and water. Divide mixture among 3 or 4 small bowls. Add 2 or 3 drops of a different food colouring to each bowl and mix well. Paint biscuits to look like moons, rainbows, clouds, and stars (see photo 4). (If coloured yolk mixture thickens while standing, stir in *water,* a drop at a time.)

Bake in a 350°F (180°C) gas mark 4 oven for 6 to 8 minutes or until edges are firm and bottoms are very lightly browned (see photo 3, page 43). Remove and cool completely on wire racks (see photo 4, page 31). Makes about 30.

1 Using a floured rolling pin, roll the dough out on a lightly floured surface, such as a countertop or pastry cloth. Roll to the thickness specified in the recipe. Use a ruler to be sure that all the dough is the same thickness for even baking.

2 Cut the dough into shapes using floured biscuit cutters, or create your own cardboard patterns, as shown. Make cut-outs as close together as possible. Reroll scraps to cut more biscuits.

3 Tuck a wooden stick under the centre of each biscuit. Press the dough down so the biscuit bakes around the stick.

4 Use a clean small paintbrush to paint each unbaked biscuit with the coloured egg yolk and water mixture.

Scottish Shortbread

6 **ounces (175g) plain flour**
1½ **ounces (40g) caster sugar**
4 **ounces (110g) butter *or* margarine**

In a medium mixing bowl stir together flour and sugar. Cut in butter or margarine until mixture resembles fine crumbs (see photo 1, page 50). Form mixture into a ball and knead until smooth.

For wedges, on an ungreased baking tray roll dough into an 8-inch (20cm) circle. Using your fingers, press to make a scalloped edge. With a fork, prick dough deeply to make 16 pie-shaped wedges. Bake in a 300°F (150°C) gas mark 2 oven for 40 to 45 minutes or until centre is set and edges are very lightly browned. Cut along perforations while warm.

For strips or rounds, on a lightly floured surface roll dough slightly more than ¼ inch (½cm) thick (see photo 1, page 70). Cut into 24 (2x1-inch or 5x2.5cm) strips with a knife or into 24 rounds with a 1½-inch (4cm) biscuit cutter (see photo 2, page 71). Place 1 inch (2.5cm) apart on an ungreased baking tray. Bake in a 300°F (150°C) or mark 2 gas oven for 20 to 25 minutes or until edges are firm and bottoms are lightly browned (see photo 3, page 43). Remove and cool completely on wire racks (see photo 4, page 31). Makes 16 wedges or 24 strips or rounds.

Cocoa Shortbread: Prepare Scottish Shortbread as above, *except* add 2 tablespoons *unsweetened cocoa powder* with the flour.

Cinnamon Shortbread: Prepare Scottish Shortbread as above, *except* after cutting in butter or margarine, sprinkle mixture with 10 drops *oil of cinnamon* (about ⅛ teaspoon) or 2½ teaspoons ground *cinnamon* and knead until smooth.

Orange-Ginger Shortbread: Prepare Scottish Shortbread as above, *except* stir ¼ teaspoon ground *ginger* into flour mixture and add 1 teaspoon finely grated *orange peel* with the butter or margarine.

Whole Wheat Joe Froggers

Legend has it that Uncle Joe was an old man who made great black treacle cookies. The cookies were named Joe Froggers because they were as big and dark as the frogs hopping around Uncle Joe's pond.

13 **ounces (375g) plain flour**
8 **ounces (225g) whole wheat flour**
1½ **teaspoons ground ginger**
½ **teaspoon bicarbonate of soda**
½ **teaspoon ground cloves**
½ **teaspoon ground cinnamon**
⅛ **teaspoon ground mace**
6 **ounces (175g) butter *or* margarine**
4 **ounces (110g) soft brown sugar**
6 **ounces (175g) black treacle**
2 **fluid ounces (55ml) milk**

In a large mixing bowl stir together plain flour, whole wheat flour, ginger, soda, cloves, cinnamon, and mace (see photo 1, page 14). Set aside.

In a large mixer bowl beat butter or margarine with an electric mixer on medium speed for 30 seconds. Add brown sugar and beat until fluffy (see photo 1, page 31). Stir together black treacle and milk. Add flour mixture and black treacle mixture alternately to beaten mixture, beating until combined. Cover and chill for several hours or overnight or until easy to handle.

Grease a baking tray. Set aside. On a well-floured surface roll dough ¼ inch (½cm) thick (see photo 1, page 70). Cut with a 4-inch-round (10cm) biscuit cutter (see photo 2, page 71). Place 1 inch (2.5 cm) apart on prepared baking tray. Bake in a 350°F (180°C) gas mark 4 oven for 10 to 12 minutes or until edges are firm and bottoms are very lightly browned (see photo 3, page 43). Cool on baking tray for 1 minute. Remove and cool completely on wire racks (see photo 4, page 31). Makes about 20.

Chocolate Cut-outs

Planning to keep these Chocolate Cut-outs around for more than a couple of days? We discovered they store better in an airtight container in the freezer.

2   **ounces (50g) sweet plain chocolate**
9   **ounces (250g) plain flour**
1½ **teaspoons baking powder**
2   **ounces (50g) lard**
2   **ounces (50g) butter *or* margarine**
5   **ounces (150g) soft brown sugar**
1   **egg**
1   **tablespoon milk**
¼   **teaspoon coconut flavouring *or* almond extract**
    Icing sugar

In a small heavy saucepan melt chocolate over low heat, stirring often. Remove saucepan from heat and cool.

In a small bowl stir together flour and baking powder (see photo 1, page 14). Set aside.

In a large mixing bowl beat lard and butter or margarine with an electric mixer on medium speed for 30 seconds. Add soft brown sugar and beat until fluffy (see photo 1, page 31). Add melted chocolate, egg, milk, and coconut flavouring or almond extract and beat well. Gradually add flour mixture, beating until combined. Divide dough in half. Cover and chill about 3 hours or until easy to handle.

On a lightly floured surface roll dough ⅛ inch (3mm) thick (see photo 1, page 70). Cut into desired shapes with 2-inch (5cm) biscuit cutters (see photo 2, page 71). Place 1 inch (2.5cm) apart on an ungreased baking tray. Bake in a 375°F (190°C) gas mark 5 oven for 6 to 8 minutes or until edges are firm and bottoms are very lightly browned (see photo 3, page 43). Cool on baking tray for 1 minute. Remove and cool completely on wire racks (see photo 4, page 31). Sift icing sugar over Chocolate Cut-outs. Makes about 60.

Biscuits and Soft Margarine

When you're making biscuits, the firmness of the dough varies, depending on whether you use butter, margarine, or soft margarine.

For slice and bake biscuits, chill the rolls of dough in the freezer rather than in the refrigerator.

Products labelled "spreads" and "diet" and products high in polyunsaturates aren't recommended for biscuit making.

Spicy Cream Cheese Biscuits

Try mixing a little allspice or nutmeg in with the sugar that's sprinkled over the tops of these soft sugar biscuits.

13 ounces (375g) plain flour
 2 teaspoons baking powder
 1 teaspoon bicarbonate of soda
 ½ teaspoon ground allspice
       or ground nutmeg
 8 ounces (225g) butter *or* margarine
 3 ounces (75g) cream cheese, softened
 6 ounces (175g) caster sugar
 6 ounces (175g) soft brown sugar
 2 eggs
 1 teaspoon finely grated lemon peel
 2 or 3 drops vanilla essence
 2 fluid ounces (55ml) buttermilk
       or sour milk
    Caster sugar

In a medium mixing bowl stir together flour, baking powder, soda, and allspice or nutmeg (see photo 1, page 14). Set aside.

In a large mixing bowl beat butter or margarine and cream cheese with an electric mixer on medium speed for 30 seconds. Add caster sugar and brown sugar and beat until fluffy (see photo 1, page 31). Add eggs, lemon peel, and vanilla essence and beat well. Add flour mixture and buttermilk or sour milk alternately to beaten mixture, beating until combined. Divide dough in half. Cover and chill about 3 hours or until easy to handle.

On a lightly floured surface roll dough ⅜ inch (1.5cm) thick (see photo 1, page 70). Cut with 2- or 3-inch (5 or 7.5cm) biscuit cutters (see photo 2, page 71). Place biscuits 2½ inches (6cm) apart on an ungreased baking tray. Sprinkle lightly with additional sugar. Bake in a 350°F (180°C) gas mark 4 oven for 10 to 12 minutes or until edges are firm and bottoms are very lightly browned (see photo 3, page 43). Remove and cool completely on wire racks (see photo 4, page 31). Makes 54 to 78.

Note: To make sour milk, combine 1½ teaspoons *lemon juice or vinegar* and enough *milk* to make 4 fluid ounces (110ml). Let stand for at least 5 minutes before using.

German Honey Cakes

*If pumpkin pie spice isn't easily available, try 1½ teaspoons ground cinnamon, **plus** ¾ teaspoon ground ginger, ¾ teaspoon ground allspice, and ⅜ teaspoon ground nutmeg.*

15 ounces (425g) plain flour
 1 tablespoon pumpkin pie spice
 ½ teaspoon bicarbonate of soda
 1 egg
 5 ounces (150g) soft brown sugar
 1 teaspoon finely grated lemon peel
 4 fluid ounces (110ml) honey
 4 fluid ounces (110ml) black treacle
 2 ounces (50g) slivered almonds
 2 ounces (50g) chopped glace peel
 6 ounces (175g) sifted icing sugar
 2 tablespoons water

In a medium mixing bowl stir together flour, pumpkin pie spice, and soda (see photo 1, page 14). Set aside.

In a large mixing bowl beat egg. Add brown sugar and lemon peel and beat until fluffy. Stir in honey and black treacle. Gradually add flour mixture, beating until combined. Stir in almonds and glace peel. Divide dough in half. Cover and chill for several hours or overnight or until easy to handle to facilitate rolling.

Grease a baking tray. Set aside. On a well-floured surface roll dough into a 14x7-inch (35x18cm) rectangle (about ¼ inch or ½cm thick) (see photo 1, page 70). Cut into 3½x2-inch (8.5x5cm) rectangles. Place 2 inches (5cm) apart on prepared baking tray. Bake in a 375°F (190°C) gas mark 5 oven for 8 to 10 minutes or until edges are firm and bottoms are very lightly browned (see photo 3, page 43). Cool on baking tray for 1 minute. Remove and cool slightly on wire racks while making the glaze (see photo 4, page 31).

Meanwhile, for glaze, in a small mixing bowl combine icing sugar and water. Mix well. Brush glaze over cookies while still warm. Store in an airtight container for 3 days before serving. Makes 28.

Gingerbread People

9 ounces (250g) plain flour
4 ounces (110g) whole wheat flour
¾ teaspoon bicarbonate of soda
½ teaspoon ground ginger
½ teaspoon ground cinnamon
¼ teaspoon ground allspice
¼ teaspoon ground nutmeg
4 ounces (110g) lard
3 ounces (75g) soft brown sugar
1 egg
3 fluid ounces (80ml) black treacle
3 tablespoons honey
1 tablespoon lemon juice
8 ounces (225g) sifted icing sugar
1 egg white
2 teaspoons lemon juice
Food colouring (optional)
Decorative sweets (optional)

In a medium mixing bowl stir together flours, soda, ginger, cinnamon, allspice, and nutmeg (see photo 1, page 14). Set aside.

Beat lard for 30 seconds. Add brown sugar; beat until fluffy (see photo 1, page 31). Add egg, treacle, honey, and the 1 tablespoon lemon juice; beat well. Gradually add flour mixture, beating until combined. (You may have to stir in the last part of the flour mixture with a wooden spoon.) Divide dough in half. Cover and chill about 3 hours or until easy to handle.

Grease a baking tray. Set aside. On a floured surface roll dough ⅛ inch (3mm) thick (see photo 1, page 70). Cut with 3- to 4-inch (7.5 to 10cm) people biscuit cutters (see photo 2, page 71). Place 1 inch (2.5cm) apart on prepared baking tray. Bake in a 375°F (190°C) gas mark 5 oven for 4 to 5 minutes or until edges are firm and bottoms are lightly browned (see photo 3, page 43). Cool for 1 minute. Remove and cool on wire racks (see photo 4, page 31).

For icing, beat together icing sugar, egg white, and the 2 teaspoons lemon juice. If desired, stir several drops of food colouring into icing to tint. Spread icing over Gingerbread People. If desired, decorate with sweets. Makes about 54.

Decorated Sugar Biscuits

10 ounces (275g) plain flour
1½ teaspoons baking powder
3 ounces (75g) butter *or* margarine
3 ounces (75g) lard
6 ounces (175g) sifted icing sugar
1 egg
1 tablespoon milk
1 or 2 drops vanilla essence
12 ounces (350g) sifted icing sugar
3 tablespoons milk
1 or 2 drops vanilla essence
Food colouring (optional)
Coloured sugar (optional)

In a medium bowl stir together flour and baking powder (see photo 1, page 14). Set aside.

In a large mixing bowl beat butter or margarine and lard with an electric mixer on medium speed for 30 seconds. Add the 6 ounces (175g) icing sugar and beat until fluffy (see photo 1, page 31). Add egg, the 1 tablespoon milk, and 1 or 2 drops vanilla essence and beat well. Gradually add flour mixture, beating until combined. Divide dough in half. Cover and chill about 3 hours or until easy to handle.

On a lightly floured surface roll dough ⅛ inch (3mm) thick (see photo 1, page 70). Use a sharp knife to cut around cardboard patterns or cut with 2-inch (5cm) biscuit cutters (see photo 2, page 71). Place 1 inch (2.5cm) apart on an ungreased baking tray. Bake in a 375°F (190°C) gas mark 5 oven for 7 to 8 minutes or until edges are firm and bottoms are very lightly browned (see photo 3, page 43). Remove and cool on wire racks (see photo 4, page 31).

For icing, combine the 12 ounces (350g) icing sugar, the 3 tablespoons milk, and 1 or 2 drops vanilla essence. (If desired, stir a few drops of food colouring into all or part of the icing to tint.) Spread icing over biscuits. *Or,* fill an icing bag no more than half full of icing. (Add 2 to 4 tablespoons additional icing sugar for piping). Using any tip with a small opening, pipe on outlines or names. *Or,* if desired, sprinkle iced biscuits with coloured sugar. Makes about 56.

Slice 'n' Bake

For a cookie wish list that includes piping hot cookies that bake in minutes, this chapter commands results.

No magic wands or silly spells are needed here. These sliced cookies, also called refrigerator cookies, give you a head start on baking. Just roll the dough into logs and chill until you're ready to slice and bake.

Then, keep the dough handy and bake up a batch of irresistible homemade cookies for unexpected guests, after-school snacks, or a break for sports fans.

Grasshopper Biscuit
Sandwiches

Grasshopper Biscuit Sandwiches

You can make the icing for these sandwich biscuits with white crème de menthe, too. For colour, simply add a few drops of green food colouring.

10	**ounces (275g) plain flour**
2	**ounces (50g) unsweetened cocoa powder**
½	**teaspoon bicarbonate of soda**
4	**ounces (110g) butter *or* margarine**
4	**ounces (110g) lard**
6	**ounces (175g) caster sugar**
1	**egg**
3	**tablespoons crème de menthe**
	Grasshopper Icing

In a medium mixing bowl stir together flour, cocoa powder, and soda (see photo 1, page 14). Set aside.

In a large mixing bowl beat butter or margarine and lard with an electric mixer on medium speed for 30 seconds. Add sugar and beat until fluffy (see photo 1, page 31). Add egg and crème de menthe and beat well. Gradually add the flour mixture, beating until combined. Cover and chill about 45 minutes or until easy to handle (see photo 1).

On greaseproof paper or clingfilm, shape dough into two 7-inch (18cm) rolls. Wrap and chill for several hours or overnight. Remove 1 roll from the refrigerator.

Unwrap and reshape slightly if necessary, then carefully cut dough into ⅛-inch (3mm) slices (see photo 2). Place 1 inch (2.5cm) apart on an ungreased baking tray (see photo 3). Bake in a 375°F (190°C) gas mark 5 oven for 6 to 8 minutes or until edges are firm and dough has a dull appearance (see photo 3, page 43). Remove and cool completely on wire racks (see photo 4, page 31). Repeat with remaining dough.

Ice the bottoms of *half* of the biscuits with Grasshopper Icing (see photo 4). Top *each* with a remaining un-iced biscuit, bottom side down. Makes about 54.

Grasshopper Icing: In a large mixing bowl beat 3 ounces (75g) *butter or margarine* with an electric mixer on medium speed for 30 seconds. Gradually add 8 ounces (225g) sifted *icing sugar*, beating well. Beat in 2 fluid ounces (55ml) green *crème de menthe*. Gradually beat in 6 ounces (175g) sifted *icing sugar*. If necessary, add additional green *crème de menthe* to make icing spreadable.

1 Cover the mixing bowl tightly with clingfilm or foil. Place the dough in the refrigerator to chill until it's firm enough to handle and shape.

2 Before slicing, check to see if the roll has flattened out on the bottom during chilling. If necessary, reshape the roll by gently rolling it on the cutting board. Slice the dough crosswise. Keep rotating the roll as you slice to avoid flattening one side.

3 Use a pancake turner or metal spatula to arrange biscuits 1 inch (2.5cm) apart on a baking tray.

4 Spread a generous amount of icing on the bottoms of *half* of the biscuits. Press an iced and an un-iced biscuit together sandwich-style.

Whole Wheat-Peanut Slices

8 ounces (225g) plain flour
5 ounces (150g) whole wheat flour
½ teaspoon bicarbonate of soda
4 ounces (110g) butter *or* margarine
4 ounces (110g) lard
3 ounces (75g) caster sugar
3 ounces (75g) soft brown sugar
1 egg
1 or 2 drops vanilla essence
5 ounces (150g) finely chopped peanuts

In a medium mixing bowl stir together plain flour, whole wheat flour, and soda (see photo 1, page 14). Set aside.

In a large mixing bowl beat butter or margarine and lard with an electric mixer on medium speed for 30 seconds. Add caster sugar and brown sugar and beat until fluffy (see photo 1, page 31). Add egg and vanilla essence and beat well. Gradually add flour mixture, beating until combined. Cover and chill about 45 minutes or until easy to handle (see photo 1, page 78).

On greaseproof paper or clingfilm, shape dough into two 7-inch (18cm) rolls. Roll in peanuts to coat. Wrap and chill several hours or overnight. Remove 1 roll from the refrigerator.

Unwrap and reshape slightly if necessary, then carefully cut dough into ¼-inch (½cm) slices (see photo 2, page 79). Place 1 inch (2.5cm) apart on an ungreased baking tray (see photo 3, page 79).

Bake in a 375°F (190°C) gas mark 5 oven for 8 to 10 minutes or until edges are firm and bottoms are lightly browned (see photo 3, page 43). Remove and cool completely on wire racks (see photo 4, page 31). Repeat with remaining dough. Makes about 54.

Buttery Almond Slices

Chop the toasted almonds into very tiny pieces—you'll find the rolls of dough easier to slice.

12 ounces (350g) plain flour
1 teaspoon baking powder
6 ounces (175g) butter *or* margarine
6 ounces (175g) caster sugar
1 egg
1 tablespoon milk
¼ teaspoon almond extract
4 ounces (110g) toasted almonds, finely chopped

In a medium bowl stir together flour and baking powder (see photo 1, page 14). Set aside.

In a large mixing bowl beat butter or margarine with an electric mixer on medium speed for 30 seconds. Add sugar; beat until fluffy (see photo 1, page 31). Add egg, milk, and almond extract and beat well. Gradually add flour mixture, beating until combined. Cover and chill about 45 minutes or until easy to handle (see photo 1, page 78).

On greaseproof paper or clingfilm, shape dough into two 7-inch (18cm) rolls. Roll in almonds to coat. Wrap and chill several hours or overnight. Remove 1 roll from the refrigerator.

Unwrap and reshape slightly if necessary, then carefully cut dough into ¼-inch (½cm) slices (see photo 2, page 79). Place 1 inch (2.5cm) apart on an ungreased baking tray (see photo 3, page 79).

Bake in a 375°F (190°C) gas mark 5 oven for 8 to 10 minutes or until edges are firm and bottoms are lightly browned (see photo 3, page 43). Remove and cool completely on wire racks (see photo 4, page 31). Repeat with remaining dough. Makes about 54.

Black Treacle-Date Sliced Biscuits

Beat in the dates with an electric mixer to distribute them evenly.

10 ounces (275g) plain flour
½ teaspoon baking powder
4 ounces (110g) butter *or* margarine
3 ounces (75g) soft brown sugar
1½ ounces (40g) caster sugar
1 egg
2 fluid ounces (55ml) black treacle
4 or 5 drops vanilla essence
7 ounces (200g) stoned whole dates, finely chopped

In a medium bowl stir together flour and baking powder (see photo 1, page 14). Set aside.

In a large mixing bowl beat butter or margarine with an electric mixer on medium speed for 30 seconds. Add brown sugar and caster sugar and beat until fluffy (see photo 1, page 31). Add egg, black treacle and vanilla essence and beat well. Gradually add flour mixture, beating until combined. Beat in dates just until combined. Cover and chill dough about 45 minutes or until easy to handle (see photo 1, page 78).

On greaseproof paper or clingfilm, shape dough into two 7-inch (18cm) rolls. Wrap and chill for several hours or overnight. Grease a baking tray. Set aside. Remove 1 roll from the refrigerator.

Unwrap and reshape slightly if necessary, then carefully cut dough into ¼-inch (½cm) slices (see photo 2, page 79). Place 1 inch (2.5cm) apart on the prepared baking tray (see photo 3, page 79).

Bake in a 375°F (190°C) gas mark 5 oven for 8 to 10 minutes or until edges are firm and bottoms are lightly browned (see photo 3, page 43). Remove and cool completely on wire racks (see photo 4, page 31). Repeat with remaining dough. Makes about 54.

Cardamom-Lemon Refrigerator Biscuits

11 ounces (300g) plain flour
1½ teaspoons baking powder
1 teaspoon ground cardamom
4 ounces (110g) butter *or* margarine
4 ounces (110g) lard
6 ounces (175g) caster sugar
1 egg
1 teaspoon finely grated lemon peel
2 ounces (50g) finely chopped nuts

In a medium mixing bowl stir together flour, baking powder, and cardamom (see photo 1, page 14). Set aside.

In a large mixing bowl beat butter or margarine and lard with an electric mixer on medium speed for 30 seconds. Add sugar and beat until fluffy (see photo 1, page 31). Add egg and lemon peel and beat well. Gradually add flour mixture, beating until combined. Stir in nuts. Cover and chill about 45 minutes or until easy to handle (see photo 1, page 78).

On greaseproof paper or clingfilm, shape dough into two 7-inch (18cm) rolls. Wrap and chill for several hours or overnight. Remove 1 roll from the refrigerator.

Unwrap and reshape slightly if necessary, then carefully cut dough into ¼-inch (½cm) slices (see photo 2, page 79). Place 1 inch (2.5cm) apart on an ungreased baking tray (see photo 3, page 79).

Bake in a 375°F (190°C) gas mark 5 oven for 8 to 10 minutes or until edges are firm and bottoms are lightly browned (see photo 3, page 43). Remove and cool completely on wire racks (see photo 4, page 31). Repeat with remaining dough. Makes about 54.

Filled Biscuit Pockets

A pleasant surprise always brings a big smile— especially if the surprise is a hidden treasure. You'll be all smiles as you bite into one of these sweet and delicious treats.

Each biscuit is stuffed with a load of sweet jams, bits of fruit, or chips of brickle and butterscotch.

For safekeeping, we suggest you store the biscuits in a secret place, because once hungry pirates smell the aroma of these gems, they're sure to raid the biscuit jar.

Sugar and Spice Rounds

Sugar and Spice Rounds

8 ounces (225g) plain flour
½ teaspoon bicarbonate of soda
½ teaspoon ground cinnamon
½ teaspoon ground ginger
½ teaspoon ground nutmeg
⅛ teaspoon ground cloves
4 ounces (110g) butter *or* margarine
3 ounces (75g) caster sugar
1 egg
1 teaspoon finely grated orange peel
2 or 3 drops vanilla essence
2 ounces (50g) raisins, chopped
3 ounces (75g) finely chopped nuts
3 tablespoons orange marmalade

In a medium mixing bowl stir together flour, soda, cinnamon, ginger, nutmeg, and cloves (see photo 1, page 14). Set aside.

In a large mixing bowl beat butter or margarine with an electric mixer on medium speed for 30 seconds. Add sugar and beat until fluffy (see photo 1, page 31). Add egg, orange peel, and vanilla essence and beat well. Gradually add flour mixture, beating until combined.

Cover and chill about 1 hour or until *easy to* handle (see photo 1, page 78). Meanwhile, for filling, in a small mixing bowl stir together raisins, nuts, and marmalade.

On a lightly floured surface roll dough ⅛ inch (3mm) thick (see photo 1, page 70). Cut into rounds with a 2½-inch (6cm) biscuit cutter (see photo 2, page 71). Place some of the cut-out rounds 1 inch (2.5cm) apart on an ungreased baking tray (see photo 3, page 79). Spoon about *2 rounded teaspoons* of filling onto the centre of *each* round (see photo 1). Top with remaining rounds (see photo 2). Seal edges (see photo 3).

Bake in a 350°F (180°C) gas mark 4 oven for 8 to 10 minutes or until edges are firm and bottoms are lightly browned (see photo 3, page 43). Remove and cool completely on wire racks (see photo 4, page 31). Makes about 20.

1 Transfer some of the cut-out rounds to an ungreased baking tray. Spoon filling onto the centre of each round.

2 Lay one of the remaining dough rounds over each round on the baking tray.

3 Lightly seal the edges by pressing the two cut-out rounds together with the prongs of a fork. *Or,* make a scalloped design in the dough by sealing the edges together with the tip of a spoon.

Overstuffed Pockets

Expect these apple-butter-stuffed sugar cookies to soften up a bit as they're stored.

10 ounces (275g) plain flour
 1 ounce (25g) toasted wheat germ
 ½ teaspoon baking powder
 4 ounces (110g) butter *or* margarine
 3 ounces (75g) lard
 4 ounces (110g) caster sugar
 1 egg
 2 or 3 drops vanilla essence
 6 ounces (175g) homemade apple butter

In a medium mixing bowl stir together flour, wheat germ, and baking powder (see photo 1, page 14). Set aside.

In a large mixing bowl beat butter or margarine and lard with an electric mixer on medium speed for 30 seconds. Add caster sugar and beat until fluffy (see photo 1, page 31). Add egg and vanilla essence and beat well. Gradually add flour mixture, beating until combined. Cover and chill about 1 hour or until the dough is easy to handle (see photo 1, page 78).

Grease a baking tray. Set aside. On a lightly floured surface roll dough ⅛ inch (3mm) thick (see photo 1, page 70). Cut into rounds with a 2-inch (5cm) biscuit cutter (see photo 2, page 71). Place some of the cut-out rounds on the prepared baking tray (see photo 3, page 79). Spoon about *1 teaspoon* of apple butter onto centre of *each* round (see photo 1, page 84). Top with remaining rounds (see photo 2, page 85). Seal edges (see photo 3, page 85).

Bake in a 350°F (180°C) gas mark 4 oven about 10 minutes or until edges are firm and bottoms are lightly browned (see photo 3, page 43). Remove and cool completely on wire racks (see photo 4, page 31). Makes about 36.

Fruity Pillows

17 ounces (475g) plain flour
 2 teaspoons baking powder
 ½ teaspoon bicarbonate of soda
 8 ounces (225g) lard
 5 ounces (150g) caster sugar
 5 ounces (150g) soft brown sugar
 2 eggs
 2 or 3 drops vanilla essence
 About 12 ounces (350g) desired jam, preserves, tinned pie filling, *or* cake and pastry filling

In a large mixing bowl stir together the flour, baking powder, and soda (see photo 1, page 14). Set aside.

In a large mixing bowl beat lard with an electric mixer on medium speed for 30 seconds. Add caster sugar and brown sugar and beat until fluffy (see photo 1, page 31). Add eggs and vanilla essence and beat well. Gradually add flour mixture, beating until combined. Cover and chill about 1 hour or until easy to handle (see photo 1, page 78).

Grease a baking tray. Set aside. On a lightly floured surface roll dough ⅛ inch (3mm) thick (see photo 1, page 70). Cut into 2-inch (5cm) squares (see photo 2, page 71). Place some of the cut-out squares 1 inch (2.5cm) apart on the prepared baking tray (see photo 3, page 79). Spoon about *1 teaspoon* jam onto the centre of *each* square (see photo 1, page 84). Top with remaining squares (see photo 2, page 85). Seal edges (see photo 3, page 85).

Bake in a 350°F (180°C) gas mark 4 oven for 9 to 10 minutes or until edges are firm and bottoms are lightly browned (see photo 3, page 43). Remove and cool completely on wire racks (see photo 4, page 31). Makes about 48.

Butterscotch-Stuffed Cocoa Triangles

Doll up these stuffed triangles by drizzling a little Icing Sugar Glaze (see recipe, page 99) over the tops.

10 **ounces (275g) plain flour**
1½ **ounces (40g) unsweetened cocoa powder**
1½ **teaspoons baking powder**
6 **ounces (175g) butter *or* margarine**
4½ **ounces (125g) caster sugar**
1 **egg**
1 **tablespoon milk**
2 **or 3 drops vanilla essence**
3 **ounces (75g) butterscotch-flavoured pieces *or* plain chocolate pieces**
3 **ounces (75g) almond brittle pieces *or* peanut brittle**

In a medium mixing bowl stir together flour, cocoa powder, and baking powder (see photo 1, page 14). Set aside.

In a mixing bowl beat butter or margarine with an electric mixer on medium speed for 30 seconds. Add sugar and beat until fluffy (see photo 1, page 31). Add egg, milk, and vanilla essence and beat well. Gradually add flour mixture, beating until combined. Divide dough in half. Cover and chill about 1 hour or until easy to handle (see photo 1, page 78). Meanwhile, for filling, in a small mixing bowl combine butterscotch-flavoured pieces and almond brittle pieces.

Grease a baking tray. Set aside. On a lightly floured surface roll dough ⅛ inch (3mm) thick (see photo 1, page 70). Cut into 2-inch (5cm) squares (see photo 2, page 71). Place some of the cut-out squares 1 inch (2.5cm) apart on the prepared baking tray (see photo 3, page 79). Spoon about ½ *teaspoon* filling onto centre of *each* square (see photo 1, page 84). Fold dough diagonally over filling into a triangle. Seal edges (see photo 3, page 85).

Bake in a 350°F (180°C) gas mark 4 oven about 8 minutes or until edges are firm and bottoms are lightly browned (see photo 3, page 43). Remove and cool completely on wire racks (see photo 4, page 31). Makes about 60.

Gingerbread Gems

13 **ounces (375g) plain flour**
1 **teaspoon ground ginger**
¾ **teaspoon bicarbonate of soda**
½ **teaspoon ground cinnamon**
½ **teaspoon ground cloves**
4 **ounces (110g) lard**
3 **ounces (75g) caster sugar**
1 **egg**
3 **fluid ounces (80ml) black treacle**
4 **ounces (110g) cream cheese, softened**
1 **egg yolk**
2 **tablespoons caster sugar**
3 **or 4 drops vanilla essence**
Icing Sugar

Stir together flour, ginger, soda, cinnamon, and cloves (see photo 1, page 14). Set aside.

In a large mixing bowl beat lard with an electric mixer on medium speed for 30 seconds. Add the 3 ounces (75g) sugar and beat until fluffy (see photo 1, page 31). Add the whole egg and black treacle and beat well. Gradually add flour mixture, beating until combined. (You may have to stir in the last part of the flour mixture with a wooden spoon.) Divide the dough in half. Cover and chill about 1 hour or until easy to handle (see photo 1, page 78). Meanwhile, for filling, stir together cream cheese, egg yolk, the 2 tablespoons sugar, and vanilla essence.

Grease a baking tray. Set aside. On a lightly floured surface roll dough ⅛ inch (3mm) thick (see photo 1, page 70). Cut into rounds with a 3-inch (7.5cm) biscuit cutter (see photo 2, page 71). Place some of the cut-out rounds 1 inch (2.5cm) apart on the prepared baking tray (see photo 3, page 79). Spoon a scant *1 teaspoon* filling onto the centre of *each* round (see photo 1, page 84). Fold in half. Seal edges (see photo 3, page 85).

Bake in a 350°F (180°C) gas mark 4 oven about 10 minutes or until edges are firm and bottoms are lightly browned (see photo 3, page 43). Remove and cool completely on wire racks (see photo 4, page 31). Sift icing sugar over gems. Makes about 36.

Perfect Pinwheels

Round and round and round they go and where they stop nobody knows.

But don't worry about this delicious dilemma— one bite will solve it. In cookie pinwheels, you'll find two tempting flavours and textures that whirl and twirl together. One is a rich dough, and the other, a gooey filling.

The results: crispy cookie wheels with a double dose of flavour.

Pistachio Pinwheels

Pistachio Pinwheels

- **10** ounces (255g) plain flour
- **½** teaspoon baking powder
- **4** ounces (110g) butter *or* margarine
- **2** ounces (50g) lard
- **6** ounces (175g) caster sugar
- **3** tablespoons milk
- **2** or 3 drops vanilla essence
- **1½** teaspoons finely grated lemon peel
- **2** tablespoons caster sugar
- **2** teaspoons cornflour
- **2** tablespoons lemon juice
- **8** ounces (225g) pistachio nuts, chopped

In a mixing bowl stir together flour and baking powder (see photo 1, page 14). Set aside. Beat butter and lard with an electric mixer for 30 seconds. Add the 6 ounces (175g) sugar; beat until fluffy (see photo 1, page 31). Add milk, vanilla essence, and *½ teaspoon* lemon peel; beat well. Gradually add *half* the flour mixture, beating until combined. Stir in remaining flour mixture. Cover; chill 1 hour or until *easy to* handle (see photo 1, page 78).

Meanwhile, for filling, in a saucepan combine the 2 tablespoons sugar and cornflour. Stir in lemon juice, remaining lemon peel, and 3 fluid ounces (80ml) *water*. Cook and stir until thickened and bubbly, then cook and stir for 2 minutes more. Stir in nuts. Remove from heat. Cool for 10 minutes.

On a floured surface roll dough into a 16x12-inch (40x30cm) rectangle (see photo 1). Spread filling to within ½ inch (1cm) of edges (see photo 2). Roll up, Swiss-roll style, starting from one of the long sides (see photo 3). Pinch to seal. Cut roll in half crosswise. Wrap and chill. Grease a baking tray. Set aside. Remove 1 roll from refrigerator. Unwrap and reshape if necessary. Carefully cut dough into ¼-inch (½cm) slices (see photo 4). Place on prepared baking tray (see photo 3, page 79).

Bake in a 375°F (190°C) gas mark 5 oven for 10 to 12 minutes or until edges are firm and bottoms are lightly browned (see photo 3, page 43). Remove; cool (see photo 4, page 31). Makes about 60.

1 Place the dough on a lightly floured countertop or pastry cloth. Flatten it slightly and smooth the edges with your hands. Using a floured rolling pin, roll from the centre to the edges with light, even strokes, forming a rectangle. Reshape into a rectangle with your hands as you work.

2 Use a spatula to spread the filling over the dough. Leave about a ½-inch (1cm) wide border around all sides of the rectangle. That way, the filling won't seep out as you roll up the dough.

3 Carefully roll up the dough rectangle, starting from one of the long sides. Pinch the dough together to seal firmly. Cut the long roll in half crosswise so it's easier to handle.

4 Cut the dough rolls crosswise into ¼-inch (½cm) slices using a sharp, thin-bladed knife. Place a ruler alongside each roll to make certain all of the pinwheels you cut are the same size.

Cranberry-Orange Twirls

10	ounces (275g) cranberry-orange relish *or* cranberry sauce with grated orange rind
1	teaspoon cornflour
13	ounces (375g) plain flour
½	teaspoon bicarbonate of soda
8	ounces (225g) butter *or* margarine
6	ounces (175g) caster sugar
1	egg
¼	teaspoon almond extract (optional)

For filling, in a small saucepan combine cranberry-orange relish and cornflour. Cook and stir over medium heat until thickened and bubbly, then cook and stir for 1 minute more. Cool. In a medium mixing bowl stir together flour and soda (see photo 1, page 14). Set aside.

In a large mixer bowl beat butter or margarine with an electric mixer on medium speed for 30 seconds. Add sugar and beat until fluffy (see photo 1, page 31). Add egg and almond extract, if desired, and beat well. Gradually add flour mixture, beating until combined. Cover and chill for 1 to 2 hours or until easy to handle (see photo 1, page 78).

On a floured surface roll dough into a 16x12-inch (45x30cm) rectangle (see photo 1, page 90). Spread filling to within ½ inch (1cm) of edges (see photo 2, page 90). Roll up, Swiss-roll style, starting from one of the long sides (see photo 3, page 91). Pinch to seal. Cut roll in half crosswise. Wrap in greaseproof paper or clingfilm and chill for several hours or overnight.

Grease a baking tray. Set aside. Remove 1 roll from the refrigerator. Unwrap and reshape slightly if necessary. Carefully cut dough into ¼-inch (½cm) slices (see photo 4, page 91). Place 2 inches (5cm) apart on prepared baking tray (see photo 3, page 79). Bake in a 375°F (190°C) gas mark 5 oven for 10 to 12 minutes or until edges are firm and bottoms are lightly browned (see photo 3, page 43). Remove and cool completely on wire racks (see photo 4, page 31). Makes about 60.

Apricot-Nut Swirls

3	ounces (75g) finely snipped dried apricots
4	fluid ounces (110ml) water
1½	ounces (40g) soft brown sugar
1	ounce (25g) finely chopped walnuts
6	ounces (175g) plain flour
3	ounces (75g) whole wheat flour
½	teaspoon bicarbonate of soda
4	ounces (110g) butter *or* margarine
3	ounces (75g) caster sugar
1	egg

For filling, in a small saucepan stir together apricots and water. Simmer, covered, about 15 minutes or until water is nearly absorbed and apricots are tender. Cool, then mash slightly. Stir in brown sugar and nuts. Set aside.

In a medium mixing bowl stir together plain flour, whole wheat flour, and soda (see photo 1, page 14). In a large mixing bowl beat butter or margarine on medium speed of an electric mixer for 30 seconds. Add caster sugar and beat until combined. Beat in egg. Gradually add flour mixture, beating until combined.

On a floured surface roll dough into a 12x10-inch (30x25.5cm) rectangle (see photo 1, page 90). Spread filling to within ½ inch (1cm) of edges (see photo 2, page 90). Roll up, Swiss-roll style, starting from one of the long sides (see photo 3, page 91). Pinch to seal. Cut roll in half crosswise. Wrap in greaseproof paper or clingfilm and chill for several hours or overnight.

Grease a baking tray. Set aside. Remove 1 roll from the refrigerator. Unwrap and reshape slightly if necessary. Carefully cut dough into ¼-inch (½cm) slices (see photo 4, page 91). Place 2 inches (5cm) apart on prepared baking tray (see photo 3, page 79). Bake in a 375°F (190°C) gas mark 5 oven for 8 to 10 minutes or until edges are firm and bottoms are lightly browned (see photo 3, page 43). Cool on baking tray for 1 minute. Remove and cool completely on wire racks (see photo 4, page 31). Makes about 36.

Choco-Peanut Butter Roll

Surround a chocolate centre with peanut butter and you've captured an all-time favourite flavour.

7 ounces (200g) plain flour
½ teaspoon bicarbonate of soda
4½ ounces (125g) smooth peanut butter
2 ounces (50g) butter *or* margarine
3 ounces (75g) caster sugar
3 ounces (75g) soft brown sugar
1 egg
2 tablespoons milk
2 or 3 drops vanilla *essence*
6 ounces (175g) plain chocolate pieces
2 tablespoons butter *or* margarine

In a medium mixing bowl stir together flour and soda (see photo 1, page 14). Set aside.

In a large mixing bowl beat peanut butter and the 2 ounces (50g) butter or margarine on medium speed of an electric mixer for 30 seconds. Add caster sugar and brown sugar and beat until fluffy (see photo 1, page 31). Add egg, milk, and vanilla essence; beat well. Gradually add flour mixture, beating until combined. Reserve *two-thirds* of dough. Set aside.

In a small heavy saucepan melt chocolate and the 2 tablespoons butter or margarine over low heat, stirring often. Stir chocolate mixture into the remaining *one-third* of the dough. Mix well.

Roll peanut butter dough into a 10x12-inch (25.5x30cm) rectangle between 2 sheets of greaseproof paper (see photo 1, page 90). Peel off top sheet of greaseproof paper. Roll chocolate dough into a 10x12-inch (25.5x30cm) rectangle between 2 sheets of greaseproof paper (see photo 1, page 90). Peel off top sheet of greaseproof paper. Carefully invert chocolate rectangle over peanut butter rectangle. Peel off greaseproof paper.

Roll up, Swiss-roll style, starting from one of the long sides (see photo 3, page 91). Pinch to seal. Cut roll in half crosswise. Wrap in greaseproof paper or clingfilm and chill for several hours or overnight.

Remove 1 roll from the refrigerator. Unwrap and reshape slightly if necessary. Carefully cut dough into ¼-inch (½cm) slices (see photo 4, page 91). Place 2 inches (5cm) apart on an ungreased baking tray (see photo 3, page 79).

Bake in a 375°F (190°C) gas mark 5 oven about 8 minutes or until edges are firm and bottoms are lightly browned (see photo 3, page 43). Cool on baking tray for 1 minute. Remove and cool completely on wire racks (see photo 4, page 31). Makes about 48.

Fancy Pressed Cookies

Appearances can be deceiving. This array of cookies is surprisingly simple to create.

No sleight of hand required here. Simply use a biscuit press to transform ordinary dough into extraordinarily rich, buttery confections.

So, for an afternoon tea or a ballroom bash, add a spark of magic with these fancy pressed treats.

Double-Peanut Spritz

Double-Peanut Spritz

7½ ounces (210g) plain flour
3½ ounces (85g) whole wheat flour
¼ teaspoon bicarbonate of soda
4½ ounces (125g) peanut butter
2 ounces (50g) butter *or* margarine
3 ounces (75g) caster sugar
3 ounces (75g) soft brown sugar
1 egg
2 ounces (50g) plain chocolate
2 teaspoons lard
3 ounces (75g) chopped peanuts

In a small mixing bowl stir together plain flour, whole wheat flour, and soda (see photo 1, page 14). Set aside.

In a large mixing bowl beat peanut butter and butter or margarine with an electric mixer on medium speed for 30 seconds. Add caster sugar and brown sugar and beat until fluffy (see photo 1, page 31). Add egg and beat well. Gradually add the flour mixture, beating until combined. Do not chill dough.

Pack dough into a biscuit press (see photo 1). Using the ribbon plate (or desired design plate), force dough through the biscuit press onto an ungreased baking tray (see photo 2). Bake in a 400°F (200°C) gas mark 6 oven for 5 to 7 minutes or until edges are firm but not brown. Remove and cool completely on wire racks (see photo 4, page 31).

Meanwhile, in a small heavy saucepan melt chocolate and lard over low heat, stirring often. Dip half of each biscuit into chocolate, then peanuts (see photo 3). Makes about 48.

1 Before you fill the manual or electric biscuit press pick the design plate you want to use and put it in place following the biscuit press directions. Then pack the dough into the tube.

2 For ribbon biscuits, hold the biscuit press at an angle, as shown. For other biscuit shapes, hold the biscuit press straight up and down. Press out enough dough so that it sticks to the baking tray but not so much that it squeezes out from under the press. Stop forcing out dough before you lift the press off the biscuits.

3 Dip half of each cooled biscuit into the chocolate. Immediately dip the chocolate-covered ends of the biscuits into a bowl of chopped peanuts.

Spritz

For a truly festive biscuit, divide the dough into thirds and tint each a different colour. Pack all three coloured doughs side by side into the biscuit press and watch what happens!

17½ **ounces (490g) plain flour**
  1 **teaspoon baking powder**
 12 **ounces (350g) butter *or* margarine**
  6 **ounces (175g) caster sugar**
  1 **egg**
  2 **or 3 drops vanilla essence**
  ½ **teaspoon lemon *or* orange extract, *or***
       ¼ **teaspoon almond *or* mint extract**
    Food colouring (optional)
    Coloured sugar *or* decorative
    sweets (optional)

In a medium bowl combine flour and baking powder (*see* photo 1, page 14). Set aside.

In a large mixing bowl beat butter or margarine with an electric mixer on medium speed for 30 seconds. Add sugar and beat until fluffy (*see* photo 1, page 31). Add egg, vanilla essence, and flavoured extract and beat well. Gradually add flour mixture, beating until combined. If desired, tint dough with food colouring. Do not chill dough.

Pack dough into a biscuit press (*see* photo 1, page 96). Force dough through the biscuit press onto an ungreased baking tray (*see* photo 2, page 97). Decorate with coloured sugar or sweets, if desired.

Bake in a 400°F (200°C) gas mark 6 oven for 6 to 8 minutes or until edges are firm but not brown. Remove and cool completely on wire racks (*see* photo 4, page 31). Makes about 60.

Nutty Spritz

These rich, buttery biscuits are like snowflakes—no two are shaped exactly alike.

12½ **ounces (360g) plain flour**
  5 **ounces (150g) finely ground walnuts**
      or pecans
  1 **teaspoon baking powder**
  8 **ounces (225g) butter *or* margarine**
  3 **ounces (75g) caster sugar**
  3 **ounces (75g) soft brown sugar**
  1 **egg**
  2 **or 3 drops vanilla essence**
    Icing sugar (optional)

In a large mixing bowl stir together flour, ground nuts, and baking powder (*see* photo 1, page 14). Set aside.

In a large mixing bowl beat butter or margarine on medium speed of an electric mixer for 30 seconds. Add sugar and brown sugar and beat until fluffy (*see* photo 1, page 31). Add egg and vanilla essence and beat well. Gradually add flour mixture, beating until combined. Do not chill dough.

Pack dough into a biscuit press (*see* photo 1, page 96). Force dough through the biscuit press onto an ungreased baking tray (*see* photo 2, page 97).

Bake in a 400°F (200°C) gas mark 6 oven for 6 to 8 minutes or until edges are firm but not brown. Cool on baking tray for 1 minute. Remove and cool completely on wire racks (*see* photo 4, page 31). Sift icing sugar over biscuits, if desired. Makes about 60.

Pressed Gingerbread Biscuits

These black treacle and spice biscuits have a cakier texture than traditional Spritz.

12 ounces (350g) plain flour
¾ teaspoon baking powder
½ teaspoon ground nutmeg
½ teaspoon ground cinnamon
¼ teaspoon ground cloves
¼ teaspoon ground ginger
8 ounces (225g) butter *or* margarine
2 fluid ounces (55ml) black treacle
1½ ounces (40g) soft brown sugar
1 egg
2 or 3 drops vanilla essence
Icing Sugar Glaze (optional)

In a large mixing bowl stir together flour, baking powder, nutmeg, cinnamon, cloves, and ginger (see photo 1, page 14). Set aside.

In a large mixing bowl beat butter or margarine on medium speed of an electric mixer for 30 seconds. Add black treacle and brown sugar and beat until combined. Add egg and vanilla essence and beat well. Gradually stir in flour mixture until combined. Do not chill dough.

Pack dough into a biscuit press (see photo 1, page 96). Force dough through the biscuit press onto an ungreased baking tray (see photo 2, page 97). Bake in a 400°F (200°C) gas mark 6 oven for 6 to 8 minutes or until edges are firm but not brown. Remove and cool completely on wire racks (see photo 4, page 31). If desired, drizzle cookies with Icing Sugar Glaze. Makes about 48.

Icing Sugar Glaze: In a small mixing bowl combine 4 ounces (110g) sifted *icing sugar,* ¼ teaspoon *vanilla,* and enough *milk* to make of drizzling consistency (about 1½ tablespoons).

Coconut-Cocoa Spritz

17 ounces (475g) plain flour
3 ounces (75g) coconut, finely chopped
3 tablespoons unsweetened cocoa powder
1 teaspoon baking powder
12 ounces (350g) butter *or* margarine
8 ounces (225g) caster sugar
1 egg
2 or 3 drops vanilla essence

In a large mixing bowl stir together flour, coconut, cocoa powder, and baking powder (see photo 1, page 14). Set aside.

In a large mixing bowl beat butter or margarine on medium speed of an electric mixer for 30 seconds. Add sugar and beat until fluffy (see photo 1, page 31). Add egg and vanilla essence and beat well. Gradually add flour mixture, beating until combined. Do not chill dough.

Pack dough into a biscuit press (see photo 1, page 96). Force dough through the biscuit press onto an ungreased baking tray (see photo 2, page 97).

Bake in a 400°F (200°C) gas mark 6 oven for 6 to 8 minutes or until edges are firm but not brown. Remove and cool completely on wire racks (see photo 4, page 31). Makes about 80.

Meringues And Macaroons

Mmmm good! That's the perfect description for these marvellous meringues and macaroons.

Egg whites give both of these cookies their one-of-a-kind characteristics.

Meringue cookies boast a light and fluffy texture with a delicate crispness. Macaroons are airy cookies with a chewy, coconut goodness.

Munch one morsel of these cookies, and you'll be asking for more!

Meringue Snowmen

Meringue Snowmen

Fun to make, delightful to eat.

2   egg whites
2   or 3 drops vanilla essence
¼   teaspoon cream of tartar
4   ounces (110g) caster sugar
     Miniature plain chocolate pieces *or*
     chocolate drops

Line 2 large baking trays with brown paper or foil (see photo 1). Set aside. In a small mixing bowl beat egg whites, vanilla essence, and cream of tartar until soft peaks form (tips curl) (see photo 2). Gradually add sugar, beating until stiff peaks form (tips stand straight) (see photo 3).

Put egg white mixture in a decorating bag fitted with a ½-inch (1cm) round tip, filling bag half full. Squeeze bag gently to form a 1½- to 2-inch (4 to 5cm) circle on the baking tray. Make two slightly smaller circles above the first circle, with edges touching, to form a snowman (see photo 4). Repeat with remaining egg white mixture, placing snowmen about 1 inch (2.5cm) apart. Place miniature chocolate pieces or drops on smaller top circles for eyes and on larger bottom circles for buttons.

Bake in a 300°F (150°C) gas mark 2 oven for 10 to 12 minutes or until cookies just start to turn brown. Turn oven off. Let cookies dry in the oven with the door closed for 30 minutes. Makes about 24.

1 Cover two baking trays with plain, ungreased brown paper, silver foil, or baking parchment. You can purchase brown paper in rolls at the supermarket, or cut up a clean brown-paper bag.

2 Beat the egg whites to soft peaks with an electric mixer on *medium* speed. The egg white foam will be white and, when the beaters are lifted out, the tips of the peaks will bend over, as shown.

3 After soft peaks form, beat on *high* speed till stiff peaks form. The egg whites should look very white and glossy, and peaks should stand straight when the beaters are lifted out, as shown.

4 Pipe the beaten egg white mixture through a decorating bag onto the paper- or foil-lined baking tray. Make three circles, each a bit smaller than the previous one.

Meringue Surprises

Buried beneath a snowy layer of meringue hides a chocolate-mint surprise.

3 egg whites
2 or 3 drops vanilla essence
¼ teaspoon cream of tartar
4½ ounces (125g) caster sugar
About 30 layered chocolate-mint wafers, broken in half *or* thin mint sweets

Line 2 large baking trays with foil (see photo 1, page 102). Grease foil. Set aside. In a large mixing bowl beat egg whites, vanilla essence, and cream of tartar until soft peaks form (tips curl) (see photo 2, page 103). Gradually add sugar, beating until stiff peaks form (tips stand straight) (see photo 3, page 103).

Drop by rounded tablespoons 1½ inches (4cm) apart onto prepared baking trays (see photo 2, page 31). Press *2* mint wafer halves into *each* drop of meringue. With a knife or narrow spatula, bring meringue up and over candy and swirl the top. Seal meringue around mint well.

Bake in a 300°F (150°C) gas mark 2 oven for 20 to 25 minutes or until meringues just start to turn brown. Remove *immediately* and cool completely on wire racks (see photo 4, page 31). Makes about 30.

Peanut Butter-Cocoa Macaroons

Store these chewy macaroons overnight in a tightly covered container. For longer storage, keep them in the freezer.

3 ounces (75g) peanut butter
1 ounce (25g) caster sugar
1 ounce (25g) unsweetened cocoa powder
3 egg whites
2 or 3 drops vanilla essence
3 ounces (75g) caster sugar
3½ ounces (85g) desiccated coconut
Cocoa powder (optional)

Grease a baking tray. Set aside. In a small heavy saucepan melt peanut butter over low heat, stirring constantly. Set aside to cool. In a small mixing bowl stir together the 1 ounce (25g) sugar and cocoa powder. Set aside.

In a large mixing bowl beat egg whites and vanilla essence until soft peaks form (tips curl) (see photo 2, page 103). Gradually add the 3 ounces (75g) sugar, beating until stiff peaks form (tips stand straight) (see photo 3, page 103). Fold in the cocoa mixture, peanut butter, and coconut.

Drop by rounded teaspoons 2 inches (5cm) apart onto prepared baking tray (see photo 2, page 31). Bake in a 325°F (170°C) gas mark 3 oven about 20 minutes or until set and lightly browned on the edges. Remove and cool completely on wire racks (see photo 4, page 31). Dust with additional cocoa powder, if desired. Makes about 30.

Almond-Orange Macaroons

What do you do with those extra egg yolks? Instead of throwing them out, substitute 2 yolks for 1 whole egg in scrambled eggs, custard, or puddings.

2 **egg whites**
1 **or 2 drops vanilla essence**
4 **ounces (110g) caster sugar**
2½ **ounces (60g) desiccated coconut**
1 **ounce (25g) chopped almonds, toasted**
2 **teaspoons grated orange peel**

Grease a baking tray. Set aside. In a small mixing bowl beat egg whites and vanilla essence until soft peaks form (tips curl) (see photo 2, page 103). Gradually add sugar, beating until stiff peaks form (tips stand straight) (see photo 3, page 103). Fold in coconut, almonds, and orange peel.

Drop by rounded teaspoons 1½ inches (4cm) apart onto prepared baking tray (see photo 2, page 31). Bake in a 325°F (170°C) or gas mark 3 oven for 10 to 12 minutes or until set and lightly browned on the edges. Remove and cool completely on wire racks (see photo 4, page 31). Makes about 36.

Macaroons

2 **egg whites**
1 **or 2 drops vanilla essence**
4 **ounces (110g) caster sugar**
3 **ounces (75g) desiccated coconut**
3½ **ounces (85g) finely chopped macadamia nuts *or* hazelnuts**

Grease a baking tray. Set aside. In a small mixing bowl beat egg whites and vanilla essence until soft peaks form (tips curl) (see photo 2, page 103). Gradually add sugar, beating until stiff peaks form (tips stand straight) (see photo 3, page 103). Fold in coconut and nuts.

Drop by rounded tablespoons 2 inches (5cm) apart onto prepared baking tray (see photo 2, page 31). Bake in a 325°F (170°C) gas mark 3 oven for 10 to 12 minutes or until set and lightly browned on the edges. Remove and cool completely on wire racks (see photo 4, page 31). Makes about 36.

Beat It!

With a little "eggs-tra" knowledge about eggs, you can turn out perfect meringues and macaroons every time.

- Go ahead and separate cold eggs, but let them stand at room temperature about an hour before beating them.
- Separate the eggs carefully—even the smallest amount of egg yolk can prevent the whites from whipping to peaks.
- Use a straight-sided, non-plastic container for beating egg whites. Plastics can retain fats from previous foods and keep the whites from becoming stiff and fluffy.

- Beating egg whites for just the right amount of time before and after adding the sugar is critical. Before you start adding sugar, beat the egg whites just till soft peaks form (that's when the tips of the egg whites curl—see page 103). If you beat the egg whites too much before the sugar is added, they won't fluff as high and will look curdled. Once you've added the sugar, beat the egg whites just till glossy stiff peaks form (that's when the tips stand straight—see page 103).

Biscuit Cones and Curls

Cheers! For celebrations and soirees, gala get-togethers, and festive affairs, these biscuit cones and curls are a *must* on your invitation list.

With a little practice, you'll soon become an expert biscuit roller. Then, depending on the occasion, you can wrap biscuits loosely for cone shapes or tightly for biscuit curls.

All it takes is one appearance and these biscuits will be the talk of the town.

Almond Snaps

Almond Snaps

What happens if the telephone rings as you're rolling up these biscuits? Hang up fast and pop the baking tray back into the oven for 30 seconds. This softens the biscuits and makes them pliable again.

3 ounces (75g) soft brown sugar
4 ounces (110g) butter *or* margarine
3 fluid ounces (80ml) golden syrup
4 ounces (110g) ground almonds
2½ ounces (60g) plain flour

Line a baking tray with foil (see photo 1, page 102). Grease foil. Set aside. In a small saucepan combine brown sugar, butter or margarine, and golden syrup. Cook and stir over medium heat till butter or margarine is melted and mixture is smooth. Remove from heat. Stir in almonds, flour, and 2 tablespoons *water* (see photo 1).

Drop by rounded teaspoons about 5 inches (13cm) apart onto baking tray (see photo 2). (Bake only 3 or 4 at a time.) Bake in a 350°F (180°C) gas mark 4 oven for 6 to 8 minutes.

Let stand on baking tray about 2 minutes. *Immediately* remove from baking tray, 1 at a time, and roll around a metal cone (see photo 3). Slip biscuit off cone. Cool on wire racks (see photo 4, page 31). Makes about 40.

1 Remove the saucepan from the heat. Use a wooden spoon to stir in the ground nuts, flour, and water.

2 Drop rounded teaspoons of the biscuit batter onto a greased, foil-lined baking tray. The biscuits spread a lot as they bake, so leave plenty of room between biscuits.

3 Quickly roll each warm biscuit around a metal cone. (If you don't have a metal cone, make a cone from pliable cardboard.) *Or,* roll the biscuits around the greased handle of a wooden spoon. As the biscuits cool, they crisp up and hold their shape.

Chocolate-Flecked Curls

2	egg whites
1	or 2 drops vanilla essence
3	ounces (75g) caster sugar
2½	ounces (60g) plain flour
1	ounce (25g) plain chocolate, grated
¼	teaspoon ground cinnamon
2	ounces (50g) butter *or* margarine, melted and cooled

Line a baking tray with foil (see photo 1, page 102). Grease two 4-inch (10cm) circles on foil. Set aside. Beat egg whites and vanilla essence until soft peaks form (tips curl) (see photo 2, page 103). Gradually add caster sugar, beating until stiff peaks form (tips stand straight) (see photo 3, page 103). Combine flour, chocolate, and cinnamon. Gradually beat flour mixture into egg whites at low speed. Stir in butter or margarine until combined.

Drop a small mound of batter (two level teaspoons) onto each greased spot (see photo 2). Spread with the back of a spoon into 3-inch (7.5cm) circles. Bake in a 350°F (180°C) or gas mark 4 oven for 6 to 8 minutes or until done. *Immediately* remove from the baking tray and roll around the greased handle of a wooden spoon (see photo 3). Slip biscuit off spoon. Cool completely (see photo 4, page 31). Repeat with remaining batter (see note, below). Makes about 30 to 36.

NOTE: You can bake up to 3 two-biscuit batches before placing clean foil on the baking tray. Grease 2 circles on opposite sides for first batch. For second and third batches, grease areas on baking tray that haven't been used.

Deep-Fried Biscuits

A rose by any other name wouldn't taste nearly as sweet as a Rosette.

Each biscuit begins with a batter that's deep-fried to a golden brown. With different moulds on your rosette iron, you can create biscuits in an assortment of shapes. Scandinavian in origin, rosette irons may be a little hard to find. Check a specialist's cook shop and cookware catalogues.

As delicate as a rosebud, these crisp, light biscuits blossom into a grand treat.

Rosettes

Rosettes

1 egg
1 tablespoon caster sugar
2½ ounces (60g) plain flour
4 fluid ounces (110ml) milk
2 or 3 drops vanilla essence
Cooking oil for deep-fat frying
Icing sugar

For batter, in a medium mixing bowl stir together egg and sugar. Add flour, milk, and vanilla essence and beat with a rotary beater until smooth.

Heat a rosette iron in deep hot oil (375°F or 190°C) for 30 seconds (see photo 1). Remove iron from oil and drain on kitchen paper.

Dip the hot iron into batter (batter should extend three-quarters of the way up side of iron) (see photo 2). Immediately dip iron into hot oil. Fry for 15 to 20 seconds or until golden. Lift iron out of oil, tipping slightly to drain.

Use a fork to push rosette off iron onto kitchen paper on a wire rack (see photo 3). Repeat with remaining batter, reheating iron about 10 seconds each time. Sift icing sugar over cooled rosettes (see photo 4). Makes 20 to 25.

1 Dip the rosette iron into the hot oil. The iron is actually a mould that's mounted on the end of a long steel handle. The long handle lets you dip the mould into the hot oil without fear of burns.

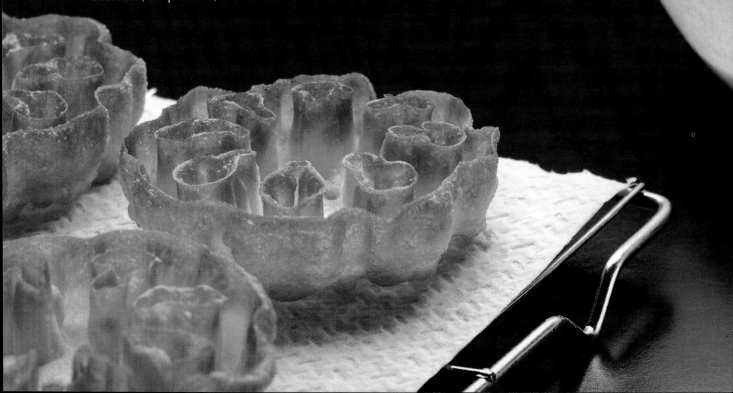

2 Quickly dip the hot iron into the batter. Be careful not to let the batter go over the top edge or you'll have to break the rosette to get it off the iron.

3 Use a fork to carefully push the rosette off the iron onto kitchen paper. Put the kitchen paper on a wire cooling rack so the rosettes don't become soggy on the bottom as they cool.

4 Continue making rosettes until you've used all the batter. Once all the rosettes have cooled, sift icing sugar over the tops.

Wild West Main Street

Hankerin' for a cookie, pardner? Meet me on Main Street at high noon.

Relive the golden days of America's yesteryear with a gingerbread Wild West Main Street. Have a chew on the cobblestone gingerbread street and yummy shop fronts. Mosey on down the centre of town and find a licorice hitching post, almond thatched shops, and a peppermint barber pole.

Everything in this town is downright delicious. There ain't a wrangler at your ranch who'll turn down this treat.

Wild West Main Street

Wild West Main Street

12½ **ounces (360g) plain flour**
1 **teaspoon ground ginger**
½ **teaspoon bicarbonate of soda**
½ **teaspoon ground cinnamon**
4 **ounces (110g) butter *or* margarine**
3 **ounces (75g) caster sugar**
4 **fluid ounces (110g) black treacle**
White Creamy Icing
Assorted sweets
Sliced almonds

Make a 12x6-inch (30x15cm) cardboard or paper pattern for the shop front. Make a 12x4-inch (30x10cm) pattern for the road. Set aside.

Grease 2 baking trays. Set aside. Combine flour, ginger, soda, and cinnamon (see photo 1, page 14). In a large mixing bowl beat butter with an electric mixer for 30 seconds. Add sugar; beat until fluffy (see photo 1, page 31). Add black treacle; beat well. Gradually add flour mixture, beating until combined. Work in the last part of the flour mixture by hand (see photo 1).

Roll dough into a 14x11-inch (35x28cm) rectangle directly onto 1 of the prepared baking trays. Place floured patterns on dough, leaving a ½-inch (1cm) space between patterns. Cut around the patterns (see photo 2). Cut 4 support triangles from remaining strip of dough. Transfer triangles to the other prepared baking tray. Give the road a brick appearance by scoring it with a knife. Score lines on the shop front to create buildings.

Bake in a 375°F (190°C) gas mark 5 oven about 10 minutes or until edges are firm and bottoms are lightly browned (see photo 3, page 43). (Bake triangles for 6 to 8 minutes.) Remove and cool on wire racks (see photo 4, page 31).

Decorate shop front with White Creamy Icing, sweets, and almonds (see photo 3). Generously ice the long, straight edges of the triangles and attach to the back of the shop front for support (see photo 4). Attach road to front of building in the same manner. Decorate remaining areas. Makes 1 building, 1 road, and 4 triangles.

White Creamy Icing: In a large mixing bowl beat 6 ounces (175g) *lard* and 1 drop *vanilla essence* for 30 seconds. Gradually beat in 7 ounces (200g) *icing sugar*. Add 5 teaspoons *milk*. Gradually beat in 7 ounces (200g) *icing sugar* and enough *milk* to make icing of desired consistency.

1 The dough will be very stiff, so use a wooden spoon, not your mixer, to stir in the last half of the flour mixture.

2 Roll the dough directly onto the prepared baking tray. Place the patterns for the road and the shop front about ½ inch (1cm) apart. Cut around the patterns with a knife.

3 Decorate the shop front buildings using icing, assorted sweets, and nuts.

4 Generously pipe or spread icing onto the straight edges of the triangles. To support the shop front, attach the triangles at right angles to the back of the shop front. Attach the road to the front of the building in the same way. Decorate remaining areas with icing and sweets.

Baking Hints

Get ready, get set, go bake cookies and biscuits! But wait a minute—not so fast. When you're investing time, energy, and money into cookie or biscuit baking, you want guaranteed success. Simply follow our easy-to-read recipes and these simple pointers, and your baking will run smoothly each and every time.

Successful Biscuit Baking

- Read the entire recipe before you start, then follow all of the directions exactly.
- Check to see that you have all of the ingredients and equipment on hand. Always use the finest quality, freshest ingredients available. Once you're familiar with a recipe, you can vary the spices and personalize it to suit your tastes. But remember that even a slight change in a key ingredient can significantly alter the end result.
- Measure all of the ingredients accurately. Weigh and gauge carefully.
- Beat butter or margarine with an electric mixer on *medium* speed about 30 seconds to soften it. Using high speed may

sling the butter or margarine out of the bowl, and low speed isn't powerful enough to cream the butter or margarine as much as desired.

● Preheat the oven about 10 minutes before baking any biscuits.

● Always place dough on cool baking trays to keep the dough from spreading.

● Bake on the middle oven rack for even baking and browning.

● Check biscuits for doneness at the mini-mum baking time given in each recipe. Use a timer to avoid guesswork.

Storing Biscuits

● To protect biscuits from air and humidity that can make them stale, keep cooled biscuits in tightly covered containers. Store bars this way or in their baking tin, tightly covered with clingfilm or foil.

● Remember not to store soft and crisp biscuits in the same container, or the crisp ones will soon be soft.

● To restore moisture to soft biscuits that have begun to dry out, place a wedge of raw apple or a slice of bread on a piece of greaseproof paper. Put it right into the container with the biscuits and seal tightly. Remove the apple or bread after 24 hours.

● For long-term storage, freeze baked biscuits in freezer containers or polythene bags for up to a year. Before serving, thaw the biscuits right in the containers or the polythene bags.

● Bulk dough, except for meringue-type dough, can be frozen for baking later. Store the dough in freezer containers for up to 6 months. Before baking, thaw it in the freezer containers.

Giving Cookie and Biscuit Gifts

Baking cookies and biscuits is twice the fun when you share the results with someone. Whether it's a special occasion like Christmas or a care package to a hungry student, an array of home-baked cookies and biscuits brightens the day for both of you—unless the cookies and biscuits arrive as crumbs! Read on and heed these suggestions for packing cookies and biscuits cleverly and for posting them successfully.

The Right Container

Half the fun of giving biscuit gifts is searching for that perfect container—one that fits your budget, suits the goody, and will be kept long after the last cookie or biscuit crumb is gone.

Containers can be as plain or as fancy as you want to make them. Ribbon-tied paper sacks or dressed-up coffee jars or cans are some of the simplest homemade carriers for biscuits. Gift shops stock many clever cardboard containers printed with bright graphics. These make delightful and often reusable gift packages. And don't overlook the ever-popular biscuit tin.

Whatever the outside container, be sure the biscuits inside are well protected from air and moisture. Even the most attractively packaged biscuits will be a disappointment if they're stale. When the container you're using doesn't have a tight-fitting lid, wrap the biscuits in clingfilm or seal them in a polythene bag before placing them in the container.

Posting Biscuit Gifts
Choose biscuits that travel well. Most bars are good senders, as are soft, moist, drop cookies. Frosted and filled biscuits aren't good choices because the frosting or filling may soften, causing the biscuits to stick to each other or to the wrapping. If you want to send cut-out cookies, send ones with rounded edges instead of points that break off easily.

Perfect Packing
Find a heavy box and line it with clingfilm or foil. Lay down a generous layer of filler, such as bubble wrap, foam packing pieces, crumpled tissue paper, greaseproof paper, or brown paper bags.

Wrap cookies or biscuits in pairs, back to back, or individually with clingwrap. Using the sturdiest biscuits on the bottom, place a single layer of wrapped cookies on top of the base filler. Top with another layer of filler. Continue layering, ending with plenty of filler. The box should be full enough to prevent shifting of its contents when closed.

Wrap It Up
Before closing the box of cookies and biscuits, insert a card with the addresses of both the sender and the receiver in case the box is accidentally torn open. Use brown vinyl tape to secure the box. (Cellophane and masking tape may crack, tear, or pull away from the package with exposure to cold or moisture.) Avoid using wrapping paper and string, which may be torn off or caught in automatic equipment.

Address the box and apply transparent tape over the address to keep it from becoming smeared or blurred from moisture or handling. And mark the box "perishable" to encourage careful handling.

Nutrition Analysis Chart

Use these analyses to compare nutritional values of different recipes. This information was calculated using Agriculture Handbook Number 8, published by the United States Department of Agriculture, as the primary source. Figures are based on the ingredients used in the American version of each recipe.

In compiling the nutrition analyses, we made the following assumptions:

- Optional ingredients were not included in the nutrition analyses.
- When two ingredient options appear in a recipe, calculations were made using the first one.
- For recipes with a serving range ("Makes 40 to 50 cookies"), calculations were made using the first figure.
- Nutrition analysis figures are based on one cookie per serving.

	Per Serving						U.S. Recommended Daily Allowances Per Serving (%)							
	Calories	Protein (g)	Carbohydrate (g)	Fat (g)	Sodium (mg)	Potassium (mg)	Protein	Vitamin A	Vitamin C	Thiamine	Riboflavin	Niacin	Calcium	Iron
Bars														
Apricot Bars (p. 22)	80	1	13	3	40	90	0	8	0	2	2	2	0	4
Butterscotch Blonde Brownies (p. 18)	140	1	21	6	60	75	2	2	0	4	2	0	2	4
Carrot Bars (p. 16)	110	1	13	6	35	40	0	20	0	2	0	0	0	0
Chewy Ginger Bars (p. 17)	110	1	19	3	55	85	0	2	0	2	2	2	2	6
Chocolate-Walnut Bars (p. 24)	150	2	18	8	60	50	2	4	0	4	2	2	0	4
Chocolate Syrup Brownies (p. 17)	180	2	25	8	75	85	2	4	0	2	2	0	0	4
Citrus-Yogurt Squares (p. 14)	150	2	26	4	80	30	2	2	0	4	2	2	2	2
Cocoa Cake Brownies (p. 18)	190	2	24	10	110	65	2	4	0	4	4	2	2	4
Coffee 'n' Cream Bars (p. 26)	110	2	16	5	35	30	2	2	0	2	2	0	0	2
Luscious Lemon Diamonds (p. 24)	120	2	19	4	55	30	2	2	4	2	2	0	0	2
Maple-Walnut Bars (p. 16)	100	1	12	6	40	35	0	2	0	4	2	0	0	2
Mocha Cheesecake Bars (p. 26)	100	2	10	7	65	35	2	4	0	0	2	0	0	2
Orange-Raisin Bars (p. 25)	120	2	17	6	60	70	2	2	2	4	2	2	2	2
Peanut-Oat Bars (p. 25)	130	3	13	8	65	85	4	2	0	2	2	4	0	2
Biscuit Mix Biscuits														
Banana Chippers (p. 55)	80	1	10	4	10	30	0	0	0	2	0	0	0	2
Carrot Drops (p. 55)	70	1	9	3	10	35	0	20	0	2	2	0	0	2
Cranberry Drops (p. 54)	60	1	8	4	10	25	0	0	0	2	0	0	0	0
Great Cocoa Bars (p. 53)	139	2	15	7	29	55	2	0	0	2	2	0	0	2
American Gumdrop Biscuits (p. 50)	100	1	13	5	15	20	0	0	0	2	2	0	0	2
Jam Gems (p. 55)	90	1	10	6	10	35	2	0	0	2	2	0	0	2
Make-a-Biscuit Mix (p. 50)	710	6	93	36	80	150	8	0	0	25	15	15	8	20
Oatmeal-Peanut Biscuits (p. 54)	80	2	9	4	25	50	2	0	0	2	0	2	0	2
Raisin Bars (p. 53)	100	1	15	4	20	50	0	0	0	2	0	0	0	2
Biscuit Tarts														
Bonbon Bites (p. 67)	90	1	10	5	45	20	0	2	0	2	0	0	0	0
Fruited Sesame Tassies (p. 66)	70	1	12	3	25	55	0	2	0	2	0	0	0	2
Fudgy Liqueur Cups (p. 67)	110	1	12	6	75	25	2	4	0	0	2	0	0	2
Mini Cheesecake Tarts (p. 64)	100	2	9	7	70	25	2	4	0	2	2	0	0	2
Rocky Road Tarts (p. 66)	140	2	12	10	60	60	2	4	0	2	4	0	2	2

	Per Serving						**U.S. Recommended Daily Allowances Per Serving (%)**						
	Calories	Protein (g)	Carbohydrate (g)	Fat (g)	Sodium (mg)	Potassium (mg)	Protein	Vitamin A	Vitamin C	Thiamine	Riboflavin	Niacin	Calcium	Iron
Cut-out Biscuits														
Butterscotch-Stuffed Cocoa Triangles (p. 87)	60	1	8	3	35	10	0	0	0	0	0	0	0	0
Chocolate Cut-outs (p. 73)	45	1	6	2	20	20	0	0	0	0	0	0	0	0
Cinnamon Shortbread (p. 72)	100	1	10	6	60	10	0	4	0	4	2	2	0	2
Cocoa Shortbread (p. 72)	100	1	10	6	65	15	0	4	0	4	2	2	0	2
Decorated Sugar Biscuits (p. 75)	80	1	14	2	20	10	0	0	0	0	0	0	0	0
Fruity Pillows (p. 86)	120	1	18	5	30	30	0	0	0	4	2	2	0	2
German Honey Cakes (p. 74)	150	2	33	1	35	120	2	0	0	6	4	4	2	6
Gingerbread Gems (p. 87)	90	1	12	4	35	45	2	0	0	4	2	2	0	4
Gingerbread People (p. 75)	70	1	12	2	20	40	0	0	0	2	0	0	0	2
High-in-the-Sky Biscuit Pops (p. 70)	90	2	17	3	60	20	2	0	0	4	2	2	0	2
Orange-Ginger Shortbread (p. 72)	100	1	10	6	60	10	0	4	0	4	2	2	0	2
Overstuffed Pockets (p. 86)	90	1	12	5	5	30	0	2	0	4	2	2	0	2
Scottish Shortbread (p. 72)	100	1	10	6	60	10	0	4	0	4	2	2	0	2
Spicy Cream Cheese Biscuits (p. 74)	110	2	16	4	75	30	2	2	0	4	2	2	0	4
Sugar and Spice Rounds (p. 84)	140	2	18	7	80	60	2	4	0	4	2	2	0	2
Whole Wheat Joe Froggers (p. 72)	220	3	37	7	110	230	4	4	0	10	6	6	6	10
Wild West Main Street (p. 116)	250	2	35	11	70	100	2	2	0	6	4	4	2	6
Drop Cookies														
Apple Pie Cookies (p. 33)	70	1	12	3	40	15	0	2	0	2	0	0	0	2
Coconut-Almond Marvels (p. 33)	120	2	14	8	20	95	2	0	0	0	2	0	0	4
Double-Chocolate Chunk Specials (p. 32)	90	1	12	5	45	40	0	0	0	2	2	0	0	2
Double-Wheat Chippers (p. 30)	110	1	13	7	50	65	2	2	0	2	2	2	0	2
Hazelnut-Mocha Marvels (p. 33)	130	2	13	9	15	100	2	0	0	2	0	0	2	4
Oatmeal Chippers (p. 30)	110	1	13	7	40	55	2	0	0	2	0	0	0	2
Oatmeal Wheat Treats (p. 33)	70	1	8	4	25	30	0	0	0	2	0	0	0	0
Old-Fashioned Chocolate Chippers (p. 30)	110	1	13	7	40	50	0	0	0	2	2	0	0	2
Rough and Ready Ranger Biscuits (p. 35)	60	1	8	3	40	30	0	0	0	2	0	2	0	2
Soured Cream Apricot Drops (p. 35)	100	1	16	4	45	85	0	8	0	2	0	0	0	2
Hand-Shaped Cookies														
Chocolate-Topped Almond Fingers (p. 46)	80	1	11	4	35	20	0	2	0	2	2	0	0	0
Cinnamon Candy Cane Biscuits (p. 60)	70	1	8	4	25	10	0	0	0	2	0	0	0	0
Citrus Kringla (p. 60)	80	1	12	3	75	20	2	0	0	4	2	2	2	2
Decorated Berliner Kranzer (p. 61)	90	1	9	6	55	10	0	4	0	2	2	2	0	2
Flaky Dutch Letters (p. 61)	360	6	26	26	200	135	8	15	0	10	10	8	4	8
Honey 'n' Spice Biscuits (p. 44)	70	1	10	3	25	10	0	0	0	2	0	0	0	0
Black Treacle-Spice Biscuits (p. 47)	70	1	10	3	50	40	0	0	0	2	0	0	0	2
Old-Fashioned Sandies (p. 46)	80	1	7	6	40	20	0	2	0	4	0	0	0	2
Peanut Butter Animals (p. 42)	170	3	18	9	110	75	4	2	0	4	2	6	0	2
Peppered Pfeffernuesse (p. 47)	50	1	9	2	30	45	0	0	0	2	2	2	0	2
Praline Sandies (p. 46)	80	1	7	6	40	20	0	2	0	4	0	0	0	2
Spicy Wheat Wreaths (p. 58)	120	1	15	6	65	20	2	4	0	4	2	2	0	2
Whole Wheat-Peanut Butter Blossoms (p. 44)	90	2	11	5	30	60	2	0	0	2	2	2	2	2

	Per Serving						U.S. Recommended Daily Allowances Per Serving (%)							
	Calories	Protein (g)	Carbohydrate (g)	Fat (g)	Sodium (mg)	Potassium (mg)	Protein	Vitamin A	Vitamin C	Thiamine	Riboflavin	Niacin	Calcium	Iron
Meringues and Macaroons														
Almond-Orange Macaroons (p. 105)	30	0	5	1	5	15	0	0	0	0	0	0	0	0
Macaroons (p. 105)	45	0	5	3	10	20	0	0	0	0	0	0	0	0
Meringue Snowmen (p. 102)	25	0	5	1	0	10	0	0	0	0	0	0	0	0
Meringue Surprises (p. 104)	60	1	11	1	15	15	0	0	0	0	0	0	0	0
Peanut Butter-Cocoa Macaroons (p. 104)	60	1	7	3	30	40	2	0	0	0	0	2	0	0
Miscellaneous														
Almond Snaps (p. 108)	60	1	6	3	25	25	0	0	0	0	0	0	0	0
Ambrosia Cookie Pizza (p. 38)	200	3	26	10	90	65	4	6	0	6	4	2	2	4
Big Chipper Cookiewich (p. 39)	210	2	25	12	75	75	2	4	0	4	2	2	2	6
Chocolate-Flecked Curls (p. 109)	40	0	5	2	20	10	0	0	0	0	0	0	0	0
Rosettes (p. 112)	30	1	3	1	5	15	0	0	0	0	0	0	0	0
No-Bake Cookies														
Chocolate Rum Balls (p. 10)	45	1	9	1	10	65	0	6	0	0	0	0	0	2
Choco-Peanut Squares (p. 8)	100	2	12	5	65	65	2	2	2	2	2	6	0	2
Cinnamon-Marshmallow Squares (p. 10)	120	1	23	3	140	40	0	10	6	8	8	8	0	4
Crisp Peanut Balls (p. 8)	45	1	5	2	35	30	0	0	0	0	0	4	0	0
Rocky Road Drops (p. 10)	90	1	10	6	15	65	2	0	0	2	2	4	0	4
Tropical Fruit Balls (p. 10)	35	1	6	1	10	35	0	0	0	0	0	0	0	0
Pressed Cookies														
Coconut-Cocoa Spritz (p. 99)	70	1	8	4	10	10	0	2	0	2	0	0	0	0
Double-Peanut Spritz (p. 96)	70	2	7	4	30	55	2	0	0	0	2	0	0	0
Nutty Spritz (p. 98)	70	1	8	4	40	20	0	2	0	2	0	0	0	0
Pressed Gingerbread Biscuits (p. 99)	80	1	10	4	45	35	0	2	0	2	2	2	0	2
Spritz (p. 98)	80	1	9	5	55	10	0	2	0	2	0	0	0	0
Sliced Cookies														
Apricot-Nut Swirls (p. 92)	70	1	10	3	45	45	0	4	0	2	0	0	0	2
Buttery Almond Slices (p. 80)	70	1	8	4	35	25	0	2	0	2	2	0	0	0
Cardamom-Lemon Refrigerator Biscuits (p. 81)	70	1	8	4	25	15	0	0	0	2	0	0	0	0
Choco-Peanut Butter Roll (p. 93)	80	1	9	4	40	45	2	0	0	0	0	2	0	2
Cranberry-Orange Twirls (p. 92)	70	1	9	3	45	10	0	2	0	2	0	0	0	0
Grasshopper Biscuit Sandwiches (p. 78)	110	1	16	5	45	10	0	2	0	2	0	0	0	0
Black Treacle-Date Sliced Biscuits (p. 81)	60	1	10	2	5	50	0	0	0	2	0	0	0	2
Pistachio Pinwheels (p. 90)	70	1	8	4	20	35	0	0	0	2	0	0	0	0
Whole Wheat-Peanut Slices (p. 80)	80	2	9	5	30	40	2	0	0	2	0	2	0	2

Index